BEEN THERE, DONE THAT

So, I Wrote a Book About It

A Military Wife's Memoir

Dana Carpenter Brown

Been There, Done That

Been There, Done That

Walton Publishing House
Copyright © 2023 by Dana Carpenter Brown

Walton Publishing House
Houston, Texas
www.waltonpublishinghouse.com
Printed in the United States of America

Disclaimer: The advice found within may not be suitable for every individual. This work is purchased with the understanding that neither the author nor the publisher are held responsible for any results. Neither author nor publisher assumes responsibility for errors, omissions, or contrary interpretations of the subject matter herein. Any perceived disparagement of an individual or organization is a misinterpretation.
Brand and product names mentioned are trademarks that belong solely to their respective owners.

Library of Congress Cataloging-in-Publication Data under
ISBN: 978-1-953993-79-3 (Paperback)

Preface

Dear Military Wife,

As I began to write this book and reflect on my life and my experiences, I thought about the wives that are married to military men and how my experiences can help them on their journey.

During the first part of this book, you will read about the journey of my life and as the book progresses, I will provide you with some tools and advice to help you. I didn't have anyone to guide me when I became a military wife. I wish I had had the information that I am sharing with you.

In the last section, you will experience my personal writing journal. I have been journaling my thoughts while writing this memoir. By sharing my story, I want to help other military wives find peace during difficult times.

I pray you enjoy!

Dedication

To my mom, Carolyn Shirley Ann Carpenter, whose soul is in Heaven.

Thank you for being an example of how to be a mother. You showed so much love and care to my sisters and me from birth until your soul left us. I love you forever.

To my sisters, Cynthia Carpenter and Felicia Blue, I love you both.

To my Husband, Tensie Brown, and our sons, DonJuan Brown and Quensie Brown, I love you to infinity.

Table of Contents

SECTION I- MY STORY

"Despite the natural belittling of one's self, the doubts, the insecurities, we have to wake up to the realization that we all write our own autobiography, we are the authors of our life story.

Realizing that, write a good story with your life and make sure to write yourself as the protagonist. Be the hero of your journey."

Yossi Ghinsberg

Chapter One:
Hello World! My Beginning

I was born, Dana Jacqueline Yvette Carpenter, in Savannah, Georgia, to Carolyn and Nelson. My mom was affectionately known as Cadillac, and my dad was called Smicky Boy. They were in love with each other and often expressed this to us. My mom was a majorette at Beach High School, and everyone in the neighborhood knew who she was. When my parents met, they began to court one another, and the sparks began to fly. However, my grandparents did not approve. It was probably due to their differences. My dad was four years older than my mom, and "wise to the streets" at that time. Despite my grandparents' disapproval, they continued preparing for their lives together.

My father would always say to us, "She was beautiful with pretty feet," referencing my mom. After my mom and dad got married, they had three children. My dad constantly reminded my sisters and I that we were products of love. I am the eldest of three sisters, my mom was 19 years old when I was born. I have a middle sister Cynthia and a baby sister Felicia.

When we were younger, my parents lived in a neighborhood project called Kayton Homes, just blocks from our grandparents' house. Only pictures tell the stories of our lives. Back then, everything seemed so perfect, and life seemed so simple to me. I remember I was very young when we moved to an apartment next door to our grandparents. Shortly after, we moved to the historic part of Savannah westside, about 10 to 12 blocks away from downtown Bay Street and River Street, in a single-family, two-story house. However, when my grandma took ill and passed away, we moved into my grandparents' home. My grandma Dora and grandpa Lester were one of the first black families to move into the neighborhood.

My early memories were like a storybook life. I vividly remember my earlier elementary school years. When the elementary school bell rang, one of my friends would lead the charge and we would raid the neighborhood looking for plum, peach and pecan trees while playing with the neighboring kids. We were just having a ball (fun time) being kids. That was during the younger and smaller golden age events. During elementary school days we walked to school from home. Our daily routine, going to school, coming back home to get our homework done, changing our clothes and then heading outside. We would stay out until it was time for us to come back in and get our school clothes ready for the next day.

Our lives were filled with playing outside barefoot and fancy-free growing up, with many neighbors that we loved and who loved us. The world was our playground, and we took time to explore it as much as we could. We lived the early part of my childhood in that house on West Hall Street.

Chapter Two:
Boy Meets Girl

The YMCA in the summer months was the place to be, and where you would find my sister and me. That was our usual hang-out spot from middle school to high school. We would go to the YMCA to beat the summer heat, and before the summer months, we used the YMCA as a place to enjoy after-school social time with our friends. Interestingly, it was also around this time that my husband said he was trying to get my attention back then. We lived in one big neighborhood filled with many people of all ages, especially lots of older children whom we looked up to and wanted to emulate. I have fond memories of those days.

My high school's name was Herschel V. Jenkins. There I met a handful of people who had significant impacts on my early life. Shirley was my first look at fashion and beauty. She inspired me to always make an entrance with my style and her natural beauty often reminded me that it was okay to have a bare face and still be beautiful. Janice, Malinda, Annie, and Kate, all inspired me to focus on my studies while at the same time having a social life at school. Rhonda inspired my attention to detail when it came to my hair and my love for hair styling. Linda inspired my love for dramatic nails that I still wear to this day because of her.

One afternoon after playing basketball, I was standing in the hallway watching the other kids in the swimming pool. I wasn't going to get in the water because I didn't like getting in the pool and messing up my hair. At some point a young boy came to that hall area. I knew him from my class. In fact, I realized we had been in elementary, middle school, and now high school together. I don't know if he said something to me or quite remember what happened but he later claimed I kissed him. This one encounter led to the unexpected.

His name was Tensie Brown. In high school, he was in my Driver's Education class and several other classes with me. One time in class he sat behind me and pressed his knees on the back of my chair. Other times he would try to get my attention by taking his desk and trapping my hair, my clothes, or anything that would hang down in between the desk and the back of my chair. He would talk the entire time in the class and give no attention to what the teacher was saying. In the Drivers Class he would come in the room with his friend and they would act crazy, run their mouths, and joke around. He would just do everything so that the class would pay attention to him however, he was relentless about getting my attention, and I did my best to ignore him.

One night I was at my girlfriend's house visiting, and it began to get dark so I figured I would head back home to get my things ready for school the next day. While walking, I saw this interesting cutie walking his then girlfriend home, and I thought, *Hmmm, this is weird. Why do I have issues with this sweet dude walking her home?* The reality, however, was that I thought he was cute, and I wanted to learn more about him.

We started to see each other at track and football practices and other sports games. He was a football player, and I was on the drill team. Before long, I was constantly thinking about him, and we started spending time together. Tensie played the field between me and his girlfriend. One night while sitting on the front porch at my house with him, I noticed two figures walking up our street. There were two girls approaching, one was a friend of both of mine and the other was his girlfriend at the time. His girlfriend was crying and upset because he was at my house on my porch. A few words were exchanged, and they left. I told him he had to decide who he wanted to be with. It would either be me or her- I gave him an ultimatum.

Tensie broke up with her and we started dating and that's where our relationship started. Growing up, receiving a promise ring from your boyfriend was a big deal. The girls in the neighborhood would have their boyfriend purchase them a promise ring and then would show off the rings at school. It was a ring promising that your boyfriend would be with you exclusively. I kept pestering Tensie to get me a promise ring. One day, he came to visit, and we decided to go to a park three blocks away. We walked to the park to sit and talk and that's when he gave me my promise ring at Forsyth Park. He finally saved up enough money to purchase me my first diamond promise ring. I was so happy.

Chapter Three:
September 18, 1983: A New Start

The two years of high school love led us to the altar. We married immediately after graduation as Tensie made plans to join the army and follow in his two brothers' footsteps. Basic training was to take place over several months out of the state. We made plans to make it happen during his break after basic training. We hurried to finalize things before he shipped out to his first duty station.

I had always wanted to have a wedding in our nearby neighborhood park after seeing a couple married there when I was younger. I talked to my mom and told her that Tensie and I would be married. She was surprised and excited for us. I started doing my research to figure out how I could pull this off within the time frame that I had. After making calls and some old-fashioned footwork I was on my way to making it happen.

I had the assistance of family and friends, people that I love and cared for who helped me bring my dream to life. The perfect gown, the perfect venue for the wedding, everything fell into place. It was everything I had ever dreamed about. My soon-to-be husband made it back home, everything was set. The whole neighborhood watched as I left home headed to the square where we would be married. A warm breeze blew as I got out of the limousine and started my journey to the square where Tensie and our family gathered under the gazebo. The music played and the bystanders stopped to watch as we listened to the pastor and repeated our vows. By then, everyone from the neighborhood had made it to the square to watch the ceremony.

"You may kiss your bride," the pastor said, and with that kiss my life was forever changed. With rice flying and onlookers cheering, we made our way back to the limo for our ride to our reception. At the reception we partied and laughed deep into the night with our family and friends and ended the night on River Street with a beautiful view of the city.

Holland

After the wedding we quickly prepared for his deployment to Holland. We had to get passports, our shots, and get my ID cards. It was just overwhelming thinking about all the things we had to do. Surprisingly, I was not afraid. I had my husband, and I knew he would make sure that I had what I needed. He would go first, and I would follow quickly behind. After everything was prepared and my paperwork was ready, six months later, I was ready for travel. I was taken to the airport by my cousin Shirley, my mom and my sisters.

I boarded the airplane and headed to Holland. It was my first flight out of the country, and I couldn't wait to be reunited with my husband, who I loved deeply. I was excited about our new life together. I boarded that plane and flew to Holland with no fear. I was curious to discover what was ahead of me and where we would live. I was curious about what the new country would be like. I wondered if I would make friends or if I would be lonely. I didn't know what to expect, but 17 hours later, I saw my husband. He arranged for one of his sergeants to take him to the airport to pick me up, and we took our long drive from the airport to the town where we would be living. It was called Steenwick. It was a small and beautiful little country town. When we arrived, my husband opened the apartment door and I anxiously entered. The apartment was totally furnished from kitchen supplies to appliances. Everything was prepared and I didn't have to do anything except put my bags down. It was beautiful, and that was the start of our lives together.

Holland was a nice place to live. The area was gorgeous. There were beautiful green tulips everywhere. It was cold in the winter but when it wasn't cold, it was beautiful. The people in the town were nice and welcoming. The military provided everything we needed. For doctor's appointments the soldiers would drive us a couple of hours to the nearest base in Frankfurt Germany. We'd have to set up an appointment with the drivers there and let them know if we needed a ride for a doctor's appointment. This was also the same for grocery shopping or whatever we needed to do on post.

Most of the time Tensie was at work and I was at home

alone. The apartment duplex we lived in was separate from all the other families. We didn't have a base; it was a small community. The place that my husband worked was a small detachment without a lot of soldiers. It was just a small building where the soldiers worked with the family members. We stayed in a regular town neighborhood in housing that the army designated for military families. We did a lot of mingling with the townspeople while there.

At first, I didn't work outside of the home, I would keep the house clean and visit Maria and some of the other wives. I also started to sew a bit and my husband asked if I would sew patches onto his uniform. That blossomed into me sewing uniform patches for other soldiers. I did that for a little while until I found a job. At 19 years old, living in another country from my family required a major adjustment. After a while, I started to settle down and feel comfortable in my new environment.

There were times I missed my family. I couldn't talk on the phone with my mom, or my sisters as I had left everybody in the States. Back then we didn't have these cell phones. We made long distance calls on our regular phone and it cost a lot of money to call, so we didn't do that very often. Every couple of months, my husband would let me call or I'd write. I wrote a lot of letters to my mom, my sisters and my friends and family back home. Sometimes it did get me down. It was depressing not being able to talk to my mom for long extended periods and that was like torture to me, but I tried to keep my mind occupied. We also made friends with Sargent Cabrera and his wife Maria. It was so nice being around them to visit and hang out.

Maria and I became very good friends, we had a lot in common. We were both married without kids. I also bonded with a few other wives. There was an older officer's wife that didn't have kids, and we became good friends with her as well. The military wives in Germany were very nice and welcoming. I didn't have a problem trying to fit in. Thankfully, the wives were not cliquish, they were very supporting. I felt like it was a sisterhood, I didn't have to fend for myself. I really needed that, especially being so young and living away from my family. The ladies were there to talk to, and over time they became my support system.

Holland was a nice place to live. Everything was simple. People rode bikes to get where they were going and there were not a lot of cars on the road. At some point Maria and I also got our bikes, and we would ride just like the locals. We rode our bikes to the market to get groceries, meat, vegetables and whatever we needed. After shopping, we would ride back home with our groceries. It was a lot of fun riding into the town on our bikes. That was the early stages of living in Holland.

We also spent time visiting with other military families that lived in the neighborhood. We planned a lot of group functions and potlucks. The husbands would barbecue, and the women would cook. After a while we moved into a two-story apartment building while we waited for the new government housing construction to finish. It was a brand-new duplex the government owned, we were the first to move into brand new houses. It was a beautiful three bedrooms and two bathrooms home with an upstairs and walk-up storage in the attic. The homes were built in a circular pattern, and we could see our neighbors from our front yards. When our husbands would go to the field, we would go from house to house visiting and having meetings. We would bake and cook all day, it was amazing. It was like living in another world.

Maria and I would entertain ourselves by taking trips to nearby posts. We loved sightseeing in Amsterdam also. We would ride on trains and go exploring. We visited the Keukenhof, a Tulip Garden with tulips planted in a row with all the colors of the rainbow. Maria and I enjoyed our time out. She spoke a little bit of the Dutch language so once we boarded the train, she would figure out where we needed to go on our adventure. When our husbands would go to the field, Maria and I would have free time to jump on the train, visiting Frankfurt and many nearby towns.

We had a chance to visit the red-light district in Amsterdam. Traveling was fun and I was not afraid. Looking back now, I wonder about how brave I was to have these experiences. She and I were buddies, and we would always be together. She didn't have kids; I didn't have kids and at some point, we decided we were going to get dogs and we brought them. I got myself a little Yorkie (Yorkshire Terrier). We would take trips with our dogs together. They were our babies at the time because we didn't have any kids.

After a few years of living in Holland, I wasn't the new wife, I was one of the veteran wives. When the new wives arrived, we'd have to make sure that they knew where to go, and who to call just in case something happened when the husbands weren't around. We were there to take care of anything they needed. Tensie's tour was for a total of three years, and we extended twice. During that time, I worked several jobs. My first was as a nail technician, I also worked at the commissary. After a while I got a job as a recreational aid or specialist at the detachment. I was the only wife that had a job back then.

Living in Holland also brought along a great surprise. We found out we were expecting our first son. We weren't planning on having a baby, but he came when God said that he was ready for us to have a baby. With being pregnant while in Holland, traveling was a large part of life, as I had to go to the nearest base to receive care for my prenatal appointments. The doctor informed me that I would need to leave at seven months, as that was the cut-off time to travel.

The military spouses were so nice and excited for me, and of course, Maria was there for me. The wives gave me a baby shower and I collected everybody's address along with their parents' addresses in the States. While I was seven months pregnant, I headed back stateside to have our oldest son. I did not want to leave my husband behind, and I feared that he would miss the birth of our son. I flew back to Savannah to stay with my mom and stayed in the house on Hall Street. Although I missed my husband, it was a happy time as both me and my baby sister Felicia, were both expecting our first child, and we were both seven months along. What a coincidence!

Healthy Baby Boy

I received the rest of my prenatal care at Fort Stewart. It was so sweet, so wonderful. However, I was bit angry in my younger days. I was always upset with everybody, and my face was always frowned for some reason. I had a little attitude. But that was just the way I was. I was not upset or scared or whatever it was just that I didn't like being bothered most of the time with anybody other than my mom and my sister. I would walk around with my face frowned to keep people away. I get my care at Fort Stewart and 30- 45-minute ride from savannah to the hospital for my appointments.

As my due date approached, Tensie still had not joined me in the states. One day as I was heading to my prenatal appointment, I stopped to get something to eat and drink from the corner grocery store. As I continued to ride down the back road to Fort Stewart, I started to feel a sharp pain. I arrived and checked in with the nurse. She did the routine check and after I was situated, she came back out and asked,

"Mrs. Brown, are you alone?"

"Yes," I responded.

"Well, I need to let you know that you are dilated 5 cm and we're going to have to send you upstairs. You're about to have your baby."

While driving to the appointment alone, I didn't know that I had been having contractions the entire ride. I didn't realize the pain was contractions. I had to go upstairs and get ready for the delivery. I calmly asked her if I could use the phone to call my mom. I told my mom I wouldn't be coming right back and that I was prepping for delivery.

She said, "Oh my God!"

She quickly rushed off the phone and she got somebody to bring her and my sisters Cynthia and Felicia to the hospital with her. She had given birth to my niece Armani two days before. After I hung up the phone with my mom, they took me upstairs and they prepped me in a waiting room. I waited until I dilated to 9 cm. While waiting I watched cartoons on television and lay on my left side eating ice chips. The contractions were painful, but I endured it. I could hear the other ladies screaming in the halls, but I laid there and bared through it.

My first born DonJuan, was born at Fort Stewart hospital. I gave birth to our son without my husband there, however my mom and my sister were there. So that was my first experience having our first baby while my husband was still in Holland. When you have your baby and you're in a military hospital they give you a minute to recover and get dressed before picking up the baby from the nursery. After I took a moment after giving birth naturally, I walked to get DonJuan from the nursery and brought him to our room. Seeing him was so sweet to me. I was immediately in love with him. I smiled at him as I watched him sleep for the first time. He was so cute in his little robe bundled up and sleeping on the bed.

By the time my mom and my sister arrived at the hospital

I had already had my baby and I was sitting up and eating. I stayed in the hospital for three days and then I went home. Red Cross notified my husband that I was in labor, and they made sure that they got him ready to come home. The army had to get him a flight to get him back home. A couple of days later he came back stateside. By the time he arrived from Holland, I was already home with my mom. When he arrived, we started our family.

Leaving Holland

When I left Holland, I lost track of a lot of the other ladies that were there and that made me sad. During our move, I lost that address book. It hurt me that I lost everybody's address. When we made that move, they moved our household items, and I misplaced my address book. Now in 2022, I have lost contact with everybody. My husband did come across Sergeant Cabrera and a couple of the other soldiers, by chance while he was out training, he was able to track them down. By the time he got in touch with Sergeant Cabrera, Maria and Sergeant Cabrera were divorced and they had one son together.

Cleveland

Once I had our first son, we moved to Cleveland. My husband was recruiting for about a year and a half. And from there, we went to Oklahoma for 3yrs and from Oklahoma to Germany. On our way back home before heading to Germany I found out that I was expecting another baby.

Chapter Four:
Career Woman, Wife and Mom

After my husband returned home, we stayed there for a month while bonding with our newborn son. After that, Tensie was selected to recruit in Cleveland, Ohio, our next destination. So, we packed our vehicle with our household goods and forwarded them to Cleveland from Holland while we prepared to start our new chapter of life after living in Holland for the past five years.

As we prepared to move, we secured an apartment in Euclid, Ohio, where my husband recruited for the army. I also decided to apply for a job on a military website named USA jobs. I was called in for an interview shortly after entering the database. I was thankful that I was able to land another job. No matter where we moved to, I would immediately go to the civilian personnel office and ensure I had my resume in the system. I loved working. This new job offered me a position with the Navy Finance Center. I wondered what type of work I would do, but being called in was a blessing. When I went to my interview, I immediately landed the job. The position was for a cash clerk working in a vault with US savings bonds.

My job duties included contacting service members by phone or mail to inform them of their savings and bonds. I enjoyed working there.

Being a working mom meant I had to find a babysitter for my baby boy. I found a lovely lady that babysat in her home. It was a convenient location, and she didn't live too far away from our apartment, which was nice. With my husband traveling outside the country for training exercises, I needed all the help I could get. I was alone with a new baby and a job in the city.

In Ohio, the weather was cold and unpredictable. Some mornings I had to get up and dig the vehicle out of the snow to get to work. I would drive in the snow trying to get from our house to work, which was downtown. Once downtown, I would park blocks away from my workplace. I had never seen that much snow before. It was a different life for me, but I did what I had to do. I worked and took care of our baby.

One morning I went down to warm up the car before taking the baby to the babysitter, and I found an envelope with a garter belt and a rose on my windshield. Somebody was watching me and noticed that my husband was not around and had placed the items on my car. I was so afraid, but I didn't tell anyone until much later. From that day on, I started paying more attention to my surroundings. It only happened once, and I am thankful it never happened again.

My husband returned home, and we stayed there for a few last additional months while he was recruiting. Then, our next duty station took us to Fort Sill, Oklahoma, for a three-year move. So, once again, we packed everything again and headed out. That was our first stateside permanent change of station site.

Fort Sill was different from what I had been used to. The area was flat, with hardly any trees or grass with lots of tumbleweed. It was a very dry climate. Once we were settled, my husband was back to work. I started looking for a job as well while I applied for unemployment. DonJuan was around three years old, and I registered him for school.

I worked as a waitress at a family restaurant, working the late shift. It was fun, but it was hard work. Carrying giant heavy trays filled with food back and forth to tables was not easy. Nevertheless, I kept that job until I could find employment on the post. The wives received preferential placement if they had PCS (permanent change of station) orders, so I applied to USA jobs to see what jobs were available. I always tried to use my PCS preference.

I was able to secure a desk clerk position. I worked just some mornings. When my husband had to be at work early or go to PT, he would bring the baby to me. DonJuan would sit in the lobby and watch cartoons while I worked my shift. Some mornings after his PT was over he would sit with the baby until I finished so we would all go home together. Working the third shift was difficult, but I took those shifts occasionally. As a young wife and mother, I did what I could to get into the government system. We established life in Oklahoma, which was a good duty station for my husband.

We also met some friends, Audrey and her husband, Sergeant Knox.

After we finished our time in Oklahoma, we packed up and headed back home with orders to go to Germany. We completed the paperwork, shipped our items overseas, and returned to Savannah, Georgia, for a 30-day leave. We drove home with the car packed full of our stuff with our baby in the backseat and headed back across the country. We also pulled my husband's 4-seater sports car behind us. We broke the trip up over a couple of days. While driving, we stopped at a rest stop to grab something to eat, feed, and change the baby. As we were leaving, my husband asked if I was okay.

"Yeah, I'm okay," I responded.

"Why is your face so fat?" he asked.

"I don't know."

"Your face looks kind of fat; maybe you are pregnant."

"Well, I don't know about that," I said.

We continued the drive, and when we arrived in Savannah, I purchased a pregnancy test. To my surprise, the test was positive. While he was sitting in the chair in the living room and I sat on his lap and said, "We are having another baby." We were both excited. Don was two, and I was six weeks pregnant with baby #2. We stayed home for 30 days and relaxed. It was a good time before we shipped off to Germany.

Chapter Five:
Life in Germany

My husband received his new assignment for the next three years. We left from Hunter Army Airfield on a 17-hour flight from Dover to Germany. We flew from Hunter to Dover Air Force Base with a layover at Dover...thankfully it wasn't an overnight flight. We waited in the airport terminal with the other families already preparing for the trip to Germany.

We finally arrived overseas and were transported to a Bomb Holder Detachment in Bomb Holder, Germany. Our living accommodations were in a small town on the economy. The economy means you stay in the local community of the foreign country you live in. The housing was also with other service members and their families. We lived in an apartment complex that sat atop a hill with a nice view. You could overlook the city from the balcony, down into the valley. The apartment was on the second floor. It was a two-bedroom, two-bathroom, typical German-style apartment.

After we settled in, I enrolled Don in the school stationed on the post. Every day we would walk down the hill to his bus stop. After Tensie left for work, Don and I would meet with the other kids attending school at the stop. During the day, I also babysat for one of the wives while pregnant. I would cook and clean until Don came back home. Sometimes I would meet him at the bus stop; other times, he would come back on his own with the rest of the kids as I stood on the balcony and watched him walk up the hill. The kids from the neighborhood would walk and play or race up the hill together after being dropped off by the bus. Working up an appetite for his snack after school, I would already have one waiting for him. I would often think to myself how good life was.

There was a small commissary and a small PX for shopping, and we spent a couple of months setting up our place. When the holidays came around, we did our traditional Thanksgiving cooking. We always kept with the traditional holidays no matter where we lived. I will always remember that particular Thanksgiving. While sitting and watching television in the living room, I felt pain in my stomach. Tensie was in our room sleeping, and Don was in his bed asleep. The pain became so intense because I was having contractions! I didn't panic; I stood up and went into the room to wake my husband so he could get him, and Don dressed.

Tensie drove us to the hospital in Birkenfeld, Germany. Most of the drive was a blur, but I do remember having contractions and hoping that I wasn't going to deliver my baby in the car. When we arrived, the nurses quickly escorted me to the delivery room after processing my paperwork. During the delivery, I shared a room with another mother. I went into labor reasonably quickly.

After my baby was born, they took him to have his footprints and weight recorded and then took him to the nursery with the other babies. With this delivery, things were different. Since he was born in a German hospital, all his paperwork was in German, and it was neat. I also couldn't bring him to the room after giving birth. He stayed in the nursery, which was scary because I wanted to bring him into the room. The hospital kept all of the newborn babies in the nursery. After a few days, they released us, and I went home with our new baby boy.

My husband and I continued to juggle family and military life and settled in Germany. When Quensie was around six months old, I enrolled him in daycare while I worked. I found a job doing nails with my new skills from Oklahoma. The shop was near the Post Exchange on the base where we were stationed. The post wasn't a regular post; it was comprised of several buildings that formed a "post-like" atmosphere. We lived on the civilian side of town. Since most wives and female soldiers didn't wear acrylic nails, I offered to do their nails for them. Everyone couldn't afford my services; however, some older wives could, so I enjoyed providing service to them while I continued looking for other employment. Before long, I secured a position at the commissary, where we did our grocery shopping. I flourished there, and I was able to work regular hours.

That was mainly our life. It was a wonderful life for me, my husband, and our babies. As long as I had a job, I was fine. I was dedicated to getting through our deployment. I worked as a cashier for the commissary, and that was fun. I enjoyed working with the employees and interacting with the service members and their families coming in to get their groceries from the commissary.

Our children also adjusted well. Our boys were in elementary school and daycare. After work, I'd pick the kids up, and we'd go home while Tensie would be in the field or at work. Me and the boys stayed occupied by visiting the local town shops. We would also meet up with the other wives who had children. The wives would gather for coffee, tea, and cakes and have a good time while our children would play with each other.

We spent a good amount of time being social in Germany. Before we left, I took a couple of road trips, including one to Czechoslovakia. Chandeliers were a big thing during that time. One wife started the trend, and the others quickly followed. Before long, we all had crystal chandeliers from Czechoslovakia. I remember the day I purchased mine. We met up for a day tour to shop and sightsee- we had so much fun! We took pictures and sampled the food from the area. Sadly, my chandelier was later destroyed during one of the moves.

The chandeliers were popular, but so were the German Shrunk (Schrank). Shrunks were originally crafted to hold clothes but soon became a focal piece in a home, hosting dinnerware, knick-knacks, and sometimes serving as a pantry. They became a big hit as many of us use them as wall units for our television. I purchased mine from Holland when

I was there. I had a house full of European Dutch furniture; I loved the rich decor.

Grandfather clocks were also trendy among the wives, but I opted not to get one because I feared it would be destroyed while in transit. By then, I had traveled quite a bit, and I knew the routine and how our personal items were often damaged. It's common to purchase beautiful souvenirs and furniture while living overseas or traveling to other states, but the reality is that your treasures don't always survive the handling.

Traveling With the Family

We headed from Germany back to the US again. Every time you move, the army gives the soldiers leave, so they can check the area where you will be, find housing, and any other things you may need. My husband didn't like to take leave; he was dedicated to work, so we didn't travel much. Another reason we didn't travel much is he had to use his leave time. The time a soldier has for leave available determines the time they can spend away.

We scheduled to take one hop per year as a family. We hopped from Germany to the States. Although it was cheap, the preparation was overwhelming. To book the flight, we were added to a waiting list for seat availability from overseas ·back to the States. The travel time was two full days. Returning on another hop was also a hassle. It wasn't a commercial plane with comfortable seating and earplugs. Instead, we traveled in cargo planes with seats against the plane's walls. It was a bit much, especially while traveling with kids. That's what those hops are like. They were uncomfortable, so we only made that one trip, and we vowed never to get on a hop to fly home again. It was all an adventure.

Our time in Germany lasted for three years. Once the tour was completed my husband received orders to return Stateside. Tensie was offered a choice of where he wanted to go. We requested to go back home to Savannah, Georgia. He chose Fort Stewart (Hinesville). When it was time for us to leave, we received our orders, and we moved back stateside after being in Germany and having Quensie there. That was the first time we had returned to our home state of Georgia. I was so excited to finally be able to spend time with my family.

Chapter Six:
Military Wife: Moving Back Stateside

We left Germany on another large commercial flight with other families flying back to the US from overseas. It was another long flight with me, my husband, and our boys. The children were getting older; DonJuan was 7, and Quensie was a toddler. After returning for a few weeks, we started looking for a home. We wanted something close to the base at Fort Stewart and started looking in the Hinesville area. After looking at many houses in the area, we decided on the area off of 31W- the main highway in town. We found a duplex that was within walking distance from the YMCA.

I liked the neighborhood because it was kid-friendly and offered things for the children to participate in. Liberty County youth services was also within walking distance. The main recreational building had a football stadium and swimming pool, which was perfect! We had finally found the first home that we would purchase. And after we purchased the house and closed, we had all our household goods delivered. Everything was delivered to us, and we started setting up our home. The boys were enrolled in school, and we settled in.

I later discovered that Fort Stewart is a base where soldiers are deployed. When we moved, I wasn't aware that the soldiers from Fort Stewart would be deployed at some point. This was the beginning of several deployments that my husband would be assigned. A year or two later, his first deployment was to Korea, with an unaccompanied one-year tour. His deployment was a significant adjustment, but I did what I needed to. At first, I commuted to Savannah, which was a 30- 35 minute drive from Hinesville. While the kids attended school, I secured a job with Memorial Hospital.

I worked on medical records, preparing the charts for the patients in the hospital. It was my duty to pull their records and to make sure those records were available for the nurses and the doctors while the patients were in the hospital or needed an appointment through the hospital. After working in medical records, I later moved to the Orthopedic Center. At the Orthopedic center, I billed medical claims and filled out claim and billing forms for the patients who came in for their appointments. I worked in that position for a while before being reassigned to a private practice doctor, where I was responsible for medical records. From there, I transitioned to the kidney treatment center. I worked at the central admissions desk for the kidney treatment center. That's where I spent my last job in Savannah until I found something close to home.

I worked at the front desk for another doctor for a little bit until I finally secured my position with Dr. and Mrs. Morris; both were doctors at the Memorial Hospital. Their family practice was at a clinic in Hinesville. I remember working with them during the morning of the 9 -11 Tragedy. *I will never forget the day the airplanes crashed into the Twin Towers.* I worked at the front desk for a few years, handled their billing, and assisted my office manager. My last position was at the Gateway, a rehab facility for patients coming in for appointments to speak with the Doctor for care. It wasn't far from my home, and I enjoyed working close to it. While my husband was away, Dr. Morris covered the cost of my home security system installation with one year of coverage so that we would have a security system. I thought it was so great that they did that for me. That's the type of people Dr. Morris and his wife were. They did whatever they could to help the employees that worked at their office.

I did my best to keep the boys busy but became lonely and depressed. I also wanted to ensure our sons knew that their dad was deployed because that was his job, and he didn't want to be away from us. So I kept the boys active and happy. My sons were enrolled in basketball and track. I traveled extensively with them when my husband was working. So, whenever they would have an event, a track meet, or a basketball game, we would travel. I would get a rental car and travel along by bus when they would have to go out of town. My husband was deployed to Korea, Saudi Arabia, and Iraq during that time. He also did another deployment to Korea. That was a very intense time for our family.

They enrolled in sports, and I also made many trips so they could spend time with our family. Every weekend we would drive to Savannah to visit with my mom, sisters, nieces, and nephews. We had a ball in Savannah. Not only did we spend time with my family, but we visited my mother-in-law, who also lived in Savannah. We had the support of our family members during all of my husband's deployments, which was a plus. Our trips were generally turn-around, and we rarely spent the night away from home. I always wanted them to be in their beds when they slept.

I was also a stickler for ensuring we were close by the phone should my soldier call. I wanted him to be able to contact his family. We didn't have cell phones back when my husband was deployed, so I ensured that I was always available for conference calls. I took great care of the boys, making the deployment easier for my husband. He was concerned about how we would be doing without him. I did my best to make sure he didn't have to worry about anything. The army was a lot different from what it is today. We didn't have Facetime and technology to keep us connected. I wrote letters to my husband weekly, and we talked once or twice every two weeks. He tried to call as much as he could, and I would try to write to him and send care boxes to him at least once a week. I showered him with mail and letters so he would know we were thinking about him.

After his deployment, he returned home, and life was pretty typical. When he returned home, we had our everyday family life, including caring for the house, having our family outings, and spending the weekend in Savannah. We spent quite a while in Hinesville while he was stationed there. My husband extended our stay at Fort Stewart for as long as possible. We had a lot of major life experiences that occurred while we were there, including the death of my husband's oldest sister.

Chapter Seven:
Military Wife: The Emergency

One incident sticks out, and when I think about it now, it still gives me anxiety. It's still hard to think about that day. It started as a typical morning. I woke up, dressed, and went to work. I was living in Huntsville, and I was working at Gateway. My sons were at summer camp.

Around lunchtime, as I was preparing to leave work, I received a call from the recreation center telling me my youngest son was in the gym playing basketball with an adult advisor, and somehow, he and the adult, who I never found out who it was, both fell on the gym floor. Quensie fell underneath him and hit his head on the gym floor. It was so loud that everyone in the gym heard it.

When I reached the recreation center from work, they brought him out of the Recreation Center. He was in a reclining seat and screaming in pain, holding his head. All I could do was recline the seat and try to calm him down. They put him in a car, and I drove to the Fort Stewart Hospital's emergency room. An attendant met us outside with a stretcher and raced us into the emergency room. I saw them trying to give him support for his neck. As a mother, I was so afraid. It was just the worst day of my life. I had never felt anything like that. I just wanted to know how terrible I was.

He spent some time in the emergency room while they stabilized him and transported him to Memorial Hospital in Savannah. I remember sirens and driving to the hospital in panic mode. Before leaving the hospital, the doctor told me he had fractured his skull. When I heard that, I feared for his life. I didn't know what in the world to do with that information. I was so scared.

After we arrived at the hospital, I waited in the emergency room as they ran tests and CAT scans. Unfortunately, the tests revealed he had a hairline fracture in his skull. I stayed in the hospital for a few days without leaving or eating. Because he was not able to eat, I didn't eat either. Quensie was alert and aware of what was going on. He wasn't eating because of the pain. All I could do was to be there to support him. I didn't want to leave his side and risk him waking up and not seeing me there.

Eventually, my husband joined us. My family- my mom and my sisters were there also. Other family and friends kept me company as I stayed in the hospital by his side. Once he was stabilized, he spent a couple more days in the hospital, and the doctor sent us home with medication for his headaches and head pain. The worst nightmare was over. It frightens me when something happens to my kids or my husband, and I may be unable to do anything about it. Throughout my life, to cope,

I would pray and have faith that everything would be okay. At that moment, I held on to my strong belief in God to get me through.

Chapter Eight:
Working Wife: Adjusting to Social Life & Work Life

It was rare to meet military wives that also had careers. Many of the military wives were homemakers. They would stay home with the kids, take care of their homes, and often didn't work outside of the home. I was the total opposite. I would be so bored staying home all day. It wasn't my personality.

I remember when we lived in Germany and how different the environment was for me. There were a large group of wives that stuck together. They had their social meet-up and set of friends, and I didn't know if I would fit in with them. Sometimes it could be a bit awkward to make new friends. I loved the sisterhood built while living in Holland, but it wasn't the same in the States. The military wives were different depending on where we lived. I must admit that it bothered me that every time we had to start over - this meant meeting new wives and families. It became overwhelming at times.

Every place and situation were different. There were a lot

of cliques of wives that formed their circle of friends, especially in the States. It seemed like the culture there, and I didn't want to get caught up. It still is like that right now, and we're retired. I wasn't the type of person that would try and fit in any else's box. I had my mindset and was motivated to create the space I wanted. So, no matter where we lived, I would always find a job to keep me busy.

The ranks were also something that caused separation. In my opinion, the men treated each other differently. My husband treated every soldier equally, no matter their rank; however, not everyone else did. My husband would often advise his soldiers, always making himself available to be a listening ear. He looked out for them and gave them what they needed to get their job done. He would also tell me that if a young wife needed help, I should call her and check on her to help her with what she needed. He taught me how to be there for others. That was his way of ensuring I didn't get lonely.

The way I dealt with the military environment was to keep busy. It was my goal to represent my husband and make sure we were always squared away. So, I kept our personal business in the family, and I didn't have a lot of people visiting my house- I pretty much stayed to myself. My husband helped me adjust as best he could, but it was sometimes difficult because of the pockets of women that hung together.

I chose not to be around women who would make me feel like I wasn't good enough or didn't fit in. Keeping a job kept me busy. I loved earning my own money to buy what I wanted or do whatever I needed. My husband took care of everything that pertained to our living expenses, and I would work and spend my money on anything I wanted. Things were good as working outside the house didn't affect running the house. One key thing I learned is that your career goals are ever-changing, and as a military wife, you have to be flexible, confident and have faith that the energy you want will return to you. What you put out is what you receive.

I enrolled in a cosmetology class to learn a new trade. I wanted to be a cosmetologist, and although that didn't work out for me, I am glad I pursued it. With my husband being gone, I had to ensure I worked around the childcare schedule. I cut my time short in the class because I was contacted to start another job. The Civilian Personnel Office contacted me for a position as a front desk clerk. I accepted the part-time job, but I wished the hours could have worked out better. I worked the swing shift from either 3-11 or 11-7. I worked there as long as I could, but it was frustrating.

I am sure the frustration also came from the pressure at home to make sure the family was functioning, with my husband's military career taking first place. I had already learned that being the wife of a military soldier required me to have flexibility. It wasn't always easy, especially being so young at the time. Sometimes I would get upset with my husband, but it wasn't his fault. He spent most of his days at the PT, going to work from there. I understood early on that if I was going to work outside the home, I had to make childcare arrangements, so whatever job I got, he would not have to worry if the boys were taken care of. I made it my responsibility to make sure that childcare was set up, so it wouldn't infringe on his schedule.

I worked at that front desk job until we left Oklahoma. Being a working military wife was a lot, especially when you're young and have children. We weren't newlyweds anymore, and I had to accept that this was our life. We worked through the hard times and figured our way as best we could.

Chapter Nine:
Establishing Finances

One of the good things about the military is they teach how to live financially and budget within your means. It took some years for my husband and I to find out how to live comfortably and ensure our bills were paid without overextending ourselves. This is something that being in the military teaches you. You learn about bills and collections. Most of the time, the soldiers have security clearances and can't have any considerable collection amounts of debt. They will even contact your husband's unit, and he will get reprimanded for outstanding bills and overdue payments.

Initially, it took some getting used to figuring out how and when everything needed to be paid. I've always had a job, so we didn't have just one income coming in; we had two incomes coming into the house. Starting out, he was just a young soldier in the military, but he's always been the type to make sure that he paid his bills; he was strict about that early on. I had the freedom to buy what I wanted because I worked. That was my mentality when we first started.

We had two different outlooks on finances. My husband wanted to pay bills, and I don't want to owe anybody, was his motto. A soldier's sergeants would have to make sure if they were single, they understood they needed to have their checking account set up and have their credit cards paid and current. If not, they would report to our husbands or the soldier's commander. Tensie continued this practice no matter where we lived. When we lived overseas, any European bills that we accumulated, we were responsible for taking care of paying those bills. If they fell behind, they would reach out.

Everyone didn't run their household with financial discipline. Some wives spent money on anything other than paying the bills while their husbands were in the field. They purchased furniture or whatever they weren't supposed to buy, and that would cause friction in their homes. I would hear the stories from my husband after his rank increased. Tensie always made sure the soldiers took care of their financial responsibility. This area is critical when you are in the military because it shows that you are responsible and dependable. The unit will pay attention to the service numbers. When they have clearances, they want the bills to be paid, and they will contact their soldier's command if needed.

When we returned to the States, we exchanged roles between us. We had to decide who would be the best person and who was more patient with paying the bills. It switched over the years. Even today, he is comfortable with me making the payment arrangements for the bills because his patience is short these days.

Chapter Ten:
Finding Housing

Overseas Housing

It can be a challenging task to find affordable housing when you're moving overseas. Military families are assigned housing that is integrated into surrounding local neighborhoods. The houses are designated for military spouses and husbands to live with all the amenities included. I had to adapt to whatever the base housing situation was where we were moving. Permanent Change of Stations (PCS), as they are called, is when you move from one base to the next. You spend three years at one location or base before you move on to the next. That was my realization when we arrived in Holland. When my husband started his active-duty tour, we had a PCS, his first duty station in Holland. We lived there for three years. Then he extended it for another three years and stayed for an additional year.

States Housing

Coming to the States, we also had to find our own housing

in Cleveland. What I liked about the options was that you could choose between apartments or housing. It comes down to your preference, what area you want to live in, and the distance you want to travel back and forth to work, kids' activities, etc. My husband and I chose to live in an apartment in a civilian neighborhood. We stayed there for a year before moving to Oklahoma. In Oklahoma, we lived in an apartment off-base until base housing was available. The service members can move on the post if housing is available. Lower-ranking soldiers were required to stay on the post because of the cost. Utilities and rent are taken care of on base. The army automatically deducts the cost from the soldier's pay. If you're above a certain rank, you can stay off-post. With the base's security and having everything on base, we decided that living on base would be best for us.

In Germany, we integrated into a regular public neighborhood. We moved into a pretty nice apartment and stayed there for three years. After that, we left Germany and returned to Georgia's Fort Stewart base. By then, we wanted something permanent that we could call our own. After living in so many places, we decided to find something off-post, with us being closer to home. For our first home, we didn't want to stretch ourselves. We had looked at many houses, but after deciding the budget, we put in our loan request application with the VA. We found a lovely duplex and decided on that one. It was a starter home type, nothing too outlandish. We also made sure that we found something close to the post. We needed something convenient for work, grocery shopping, and a good school for the boys.

When shopping for a home, it is vital that you pay attention to what you're spending, whether it's renting or buying. For us paying a mortgage ended up being a benefit to us. We now have property that we own not too far from our home, where we have family. Some of these decisions you must make when looking for housing will depend on what you can afford. The location is also another very important aspect to consider. We always tried to make sure that we had access to the base for groceries and health care. Everything worked out for us. We lived in our first home for many years.

Later on, we moved to Fort Knox in Kentucky. We stayed on post to have access to the schools for our youngest son. We felt that the school system was better on post up until my husband retired. Once he retired, we found housing off-post. It was a condo in a new golf community. Our application was approved, and we moved into a brand-new condo. We stayed there until our youngest son graduated from college.

I thought that buying another house would be a great option for us. With me having my job and my husband being retired, he decided to start working another job, and we started looking for houses. It was tedious because now I had a larger pool of houses to choose from. It took me a while before I found our second purchase. I found a realtor through one of my girlfriends that I worked with. She used the same person to find her house, so I chose to work with her.

We searched for homes in different neighborhoods until I found the right place. We found a home in a beautiful neighborhood that was just a short distance from shopping and not too far from work and post. Our goal was to be close to the post and not break the bank. It was a learning experience going out and trying to narrow down our choices with pros and cons on each option. We found that it equals itself out; if you stay on post or off, you will pay all at once or separately. A certain amount is available through your BAQ (Basic Allowance for Quarters) deduction on post or out-of-pocket off-base.

When looking for a home, you should keep in mind these key points:

> ➤ The area (neighborhood)

> ➤ How much you're willing to spend.

> ➤ How far of a commute you're going to have to drive to work.

> ➤ Shopping

> ➤ Childcare if your kids go to school on base and you work off base.

The answers to this list should help direct you in deciding on the best housing options for your family.

Chapter Eleven:
Raising Children

Raising children while a parent is deployed can be hard, but you can do it if you establish a routine for your family. Small babies won't understand that dad or mom is deployed. When they get a little older, they'll ask questions. I remember my son saying, "Dad isn't coming home?" When they would get out of school or would notice that he wasn't there when they got out of bed. You will notice that the children will become sad, so as parents, you have to be prepared to answer their questions and keep them at peace.

Raising children takes the support of two parents. Although my husband wasn't home often, he made sure the boys took care of me and respected me. One day I talked with my oldest son, and he mentioned to me that he took what his dad said to heart. Whenever he had to leave, go out to the field, or was deployed, my husband told him, "You're the man of the house, take care of your mom." Hearing that made me smile.

I did the best I could to keep them busy. My solution was to keep them happy and busy. My oldest son became my little traveling buddy when they grew up a little older. Everywhere I went, I took him with me. We spent a lot of time out of the house. I was adamant about him only staying with my family members, like my mom or sisters. He didn't spend the night out unless it was with family. After Quensie was born, I would pack them up and spend as much time out with them as possible to burn off their energy.

Every weekend we spent time going on different adventures. If my husband wasn't available, I would take them to the bowling alley or skating rink and head out with a car full of kids. My sisters and I would take all our kids to the movies. We'd get everybody on the weekend and go as a family. I would always take them, and we'd go somewhere to get their minds off where Daddy was. It worked out well for us.

They both enjoyed being outside and in the fresh air. It's good for the babies to be outside when the weather permits. When we were at home, they would spend most of their time watching TV or playing games with their toys. I wanted them to explore the outside. Being in the sun, running in the grass, and playing outside kept them active, and it was much healthier for them. I made sure to think about what they might be going through. I enjoyed time out also, and it also gave me peace.

After work, I would pick the boys up, cook them something to eat, and then head out to whatever sporting event I had them sign up for. They were summer camp regulars. During the summer, they were always signed up for summer camp to keep them on a routine when they didn't have school, so they weren't sitting around the house. They'd get up and get cleaned up, eat, clean the house, and I'd take them to summer camp. I still wanted to work, and most of the time, their dad had things he had to do on the weekend for work. Then, once he was done, we would head out to do family activities if he was home.

I had to be on full alert raising boys. I remember one time our oldest would not do his homework and was getting in trouble in school. I didn't find out about it because when the teacher or the principal would leave messages on my voicemail, I didn't receive them. My son decided to erase the messages off the phone so I wouldn't know he had gotten in trouble. Thankfully, my youngest was pretty low-key. So, it was a good balance raising the two of them.

I didn't have to worry about them. My goal was to keep their little minds occupied. They would get together and figure out what they wanted to do. They would get one over on me if they were bored at home and I was napping. They didn't do that too much because they knew what they could get away with. They were never into one particular thing. They'd go to the pool and spend time in the swimming pool right down the street. I used to let my sons ride their bikes down to the recreation center after completing their homework and chores.

Once the summer camp was over, they stayed in the park by the track field area. They would play with the other kids, ride their bikes, and skateboard, all those things they had to occupy them outside. Overseas my oldest son's school would take the kids on field trips. He attended school with German students, and he learned a little bit of German back then.

Although I did what I could, we still missed having my husband home with us. There were those moments when I wished he was home. We all missed him. But in those times, he would call us. It's like he was able to feel how we felt. When I finally got a cell phone, and he was able to call us, he would call on the cell phone at the right time to talk to us, making everybody feel better.

To stay connected, the kids constantly wrote him letters and sent him small items in his care packages we would make for him. I decided that he would not feel alone when he was deployed and going to the field. He would know that we loved and missed him. If he went out for just two weeks or a month, we didn't send any care packages because they would be in the area, but if he was deployed, we kept up with the letters and care packages.

Currently, my youngest is deployed, and the care packages help keep his morale up when he knows he will get something in the mail. I am old school, so I still write him letters and put boxes in the mail with the items I come across at the commissary or the PX. I send him things I know he will need, just like we did with his father.

SECTION II- LESSONS LEARNED

"Reflective thinking turns experience into insight."
John C. Maxell

Chapter Twelve:
Advice to My Younger Self

Growing up, I wanted to do something more with my life. I didn't want to live in Savannah and work every day without a future. My husband played a crucial role in letting me see that there was something other than staying home and living a routine life. Traveling with him, I was able to experience another side of life. Growing up, I dreamed of getting my cosmetology license, working for someone in a shop, and eventually having my own beauty shop. Those were my initial thoughts about what I wanted to do with my life. I didn't have an interest in going to college. I wanted to be a beautician.

Instead, I married a soldier right after my high school graduation. The military life took over, and because I didn't know where we would be stationed or what the job market would be like, I put my plans on hold. When living in a different place, you must research the area and plan from there. Since I was living overseas, there was no way I could attend Beauty School.

Advice to My Younger Self

Be Confident!

Leaving to go out into the world as a young married military wife, I would now tell my younger self to be comfortable in your skin. Having confidence, and trying your best to be as authentic as you can with who you are, is something I believe in. We should never pretend to be something that we're not. I used to have self-esteem issues that affected my confidence. I remember becoming self-conscious about my weight while being around the other military wives. Things were different when I left Holland and returned to the States. Being back in the US exposed me to the range of ranks that our husbands had to work within. There were social functions where the wives would be there alongside their husbands, and for the first time after having the baby, I felt very self-conscious about my weight. I didn't have much self-confidence, and rebuilding my confidence took me a while.

Don't Neglect Your Career

Not having a full-time career for myself bothered me. I felt like I needed to do better. Sometimes I would become angry that my husband would leave so often, and I would be there raising the kids. At the time, I didn't always appreciate the life experience I gained from living in different places and working different jobs. But this deep reflection makes me thankful for how our lives turned out. Because of being with a military spouse, I have experienced different jobs that I would not have typically done. In addition, moving around so much allowed me to have an extensive experience in various careers and job sectors. My resume included various wonderful jobs ranging from recreational aid, nail technician, cashier, waitress, front desk clerk, and vault clerk. It also included my position as an assistant manager for a doctor's office.

Today I work in civil service, and I've been working this job that I have now for several years. I've been in the system for over 15 years. I am also proud that I could get into government service and secure a contract. I endured the lengthy process. To be eligible, you must have no criminal record, your papers completed for clearance, and a background check. My introduction to civil service was when I decided to apply for a job in the hospital after my family relocated to Kentucky. I applied with a supervisor of a civilian company that handled contract positions within the hospital at Fort Knox. I knew about contracts from my previous job at Fort Stewart, so when I talked to the supervisor, I was confident that I was the person for the position. In life, you must be confident, ask for what you want and not be afraid.

When I approached the supervisor, she seemed to be waiting for me to get there. After we talked, I asked her to keep me in mind. Within a month, she called me.

She said, "I'm going to stick my neck out and put you in this job."

To this day, she is one of my favorite people that I have come across at Fort Knox. She gave me a chance to work as a contractor. My old supervisor was another that took a chance on me. She's retired now, but she was another person that I loved who got me into government service. Once you're in government service, the sky's the limit. You can get course training, a TDY (Temporary Duty Travel) to training, for some you travel on your job. You can do so much once you get into government service. I thank God that I have always been lucky to get jobs that I liked. I believe it's because I go in with my mindset, knowing what I would like to do. I know what makes me happy. Working in retail selling clothes is another thing that I love. I am good at selling clothes and jewelry.

Getting in the system has been life changing. My son mentioned to me that he remembered me telling him I would get into the system. I used to talk to him like he was a grown person. He was always mature and would listen to what I told him. I like to talk to him now because he's intelligent. He remembers me telling him how much we made and said he thought we were rich. "We just know how to deal with the money we earn; we are not rich," I said.

The path that I'm on now is more diverse. I can do any job, and I enjoy it. I don't have any problems that would distract me or keep me from being dependable or reliable. I take my work seriously. I can't say I have worked my dream job yet, but it's always possible for me to do what I love. I can still get my certification in the different areas of cosmetology, which I will be working on in the foreseeable future. Maybe one day I will open that salon. Who knows what the future holds for me. But I know that I would not have changed any career or job I've had throughout the military. It's made me into the person that I am. Although I didn't attend college, I have knowledge from my on-the-job training. Although I'm not in the military, I consider myself a high-ranking officer. I have the experience of one. I'm not saying that to brag; that's how I feel.

I'm just thankful. I am at a place right now where I can reflect. Even before I married my husband, I can also see the military played a role in my life. In Savannah, I was raised near Hunter Army Airfield, which is a major base in Savannah. I also remember my grandfather used to like to watch war movies. While I was young, I was always watching military movies. I had a fascination with the military when I was young because of him. Then to top it off, my Uncle Vernon, one of the best people I could ever have, is a retired army soldier. It's as if God was sending me signs and messages before I even realized that would be my path.

Don't Give Up on Your Dreams!

Stay focused on what you want to do as far as your career and your life. Never give up on your dreams. Always have faith and work towards what it is that you want.

Step Out of Your Comfort Zone!

Be patient and don't be afraid to step out of your comfort zone. Do something different that you've never done. Remember that no job can be beneath you, and you should never look down on anyone because of what they are doing to earn an income. Whatever that person is doing means a lot to them and brings money into their families. Respect people, no matter what level they are on.

Be Kind!

Be thankful, grateful, and be kind to others along the way. Be as nice as you can to others. What you give out is what you receive. I've learned this over the years. You shouldn't have a bad attitude and talk to people and disrespect others if you want good things to happen to you. That is not the way life works. If you put out bad vibes, bad vibes are what you will get back. I didn't always know how to do this, but I see life from a different perspective as I grow. I make it my business to be positive. I do what feels good to my spirit, keeping my heart full and walking in faith.

I am being faithful in loving myself and being as pleasant as possible. No one deserves disrespect, so I keep all negative vibes away. I also believe that if I am not mistreating anybody, my good vibrations will go out to my family. I would not want anyone to mistreat my sons, grandchildren, and other family members. I want the people dealing with them to treat them kindly.

Stay Connected to Family

I want my life and story to help others. We all go through life situations for a reason, and I realize that I am where I am now because of my experiences. My husband, my sons, my mom, my dad, my sisters, and all my family members made me the person I am. I believe that we should always keep this bond with our family no matter where we go in life. So don't push your family away. If you need to talk, talk to your family. If you need to talk, talk to your husband.

Talk to Someone

We spent the first five years married before we had kids. It was just me and my husband. I was away from everybody, and I kept a lot of emotions inside. I didn't want to bother him because I knew how hard he had to work. I knew it was challenging to be a soldier in the military. I wanted to make it easier for him, so I kept a lot of stuff bottled up, but truthfully it made me bitter for a very long time. I had to figure out how to eliminate all my negative energy. I never want to return to that dark place again. That has become a part of my purpose in life, to make sure I am thankful and happy. I always thank God, stay active, and get outside to get fresh air while I am living my life.

Recently I helped my daughter-in-law pack up their entire home because my youngest son is currently deployed in the military. So, it's her and the baby. I saw myself as I watched her, and it moved me in a way I cannot explain. It was like the younger version of my life flashed before me. I needed to see this in real-time to see what I went through. I watched her family rally around to help her and my grandbaby get her settled into their new home. It was so great to experience. I was able to release a lot of pinned-up emotions. I was able to put a visual in my brain of the things that I went through. At the time, I didn't assess the magnitude of the situation because I was busy living life and surviving the best way I knew how.

Our oldest son and his wife have two kids. I observe how they balance having a baby and a five-year-old. It's like our story is replaying itself all over again but from another perspective. The grandkids are all growing up together for a time with their cousins. What a sight to behold. All three have three different personalities, and each baby holds that special place I have for them in my heart.

My trips home enlighten me, and they tell me I'm doing exactly what I need to do. At this time in my life, I'm so happy for today and what it holds. I love my husband and sons with all my heart. Because of them, I am the person that I am. My mom, dad, sisters, cousin, and the people I grew up with in my neighborhood all contributed. They all help you, and you only know that they're helping you once you get older and you look back and see that you emulate some parts of them somehow.

Those people have something to do with who you are at the end of the day. All the good and bad stuff that we get is a blessing. A blessing or a lesson. To be who you are, the age you are, the color you are, who you're married to, what your kids are like- everything is a reflection of you and what you contributed to them for them to give back to you. I'm grateful and it's amazing to me. It's so many people out in the world. If I help one person, that will mean the world to me. I understand it will be okay if we don't dread anything coming into our life because everything happens for a reason, and you are where you are, where you're supposed to be. Buckle Up. It's going to be what you make it.

Chapter Thirteen:
Lessons Learned

I learned a lot about myself after decades as a military wife. When I meet other wives, I give them pointers to help them overcome some of the challenges. As I wrote this book, I thought about what I did to get through my challenges. This chapters entails some of those lessons.

Ask for help!

Don't try and figure things out on your own. If you are in a situation and you're away from your family and you're young, and you're scared, you may have children or you may not, find someone that you can trust that can help you when needed. Find someone that you can trust that will not tell anyone your personal business. Just don't keep it all in. It's best that you have somebody to help you if you want to talk and listen and give you advice on certain things. Get a Battle Buddy:

Have someone that you can call that can come and help you or can talk to you or whatever when you don't have your spouse with you. I remember when I found my battle buddy. In Germany I came across a couple of wives whose husbands were friends with my husband. They worked together so we became friends. One of the wives worked at the daycare with me, and we became good friends. This helped me out when I felt lonely and missed being with my family.

Become a Problem Solver

Make sure that you learn how to be a good analytical person, because if something happens to you, you want to be able to understand how to handle it. There will be situations that arise when your husband is deployed or in the field and if you do not understand how to handle things you'll be stuck. You will get frustrated and upset because your husband's not around. You must go through all this. Not having my husband around all the time caused me to use my critical thinking skills. Eventually those situations made me stronger. I learned how to work out my problems by finding a solution to work out whatever was happening.

Stay Busy

It is up to you to find something to do to stay busy. I suggest you either find a job or go out and find an activity with a wives' club. As I mentioned earlier, I also enrolled in cosmetology class to learn a new trade. I wanted to be a cosmetologist but with my husband gone, that plan did not work out for me. I had to make sure I worked around the childcare schedule. I had to cut my time in the course short because I was contacted for another job. The Civilian Personnel Office contacted me for a position as a front desk clerk. I accepted the part-time job, but the hours again were not ideal. I worked Swing shift 3-11,11-7. I worked there as long as I could. I must admit I was frustrated while working there. I am sure the frustration also came from the pressure at home to make sure the family was functioning, with my husband's military career taking first place.

Be Flexible

One of the biggest lessons I learned as the wife of a military soldier was to be flexible.

It wasn't always easy, especially being so young at the time. Sometimes I would get upset with my husband, but it wasn't his fault. He spent most of his days at the PT and then from there he would go to work. I understood early on that if I was going to work outside the home, I had to make arrangements for childcare, so whatever job that I decided to get he would not have to worry if the boys were taken care of. In fact, I made it my responsibility to make sure that childcare was set up, so it wouldn't infringe on his schedule.

Keep Check of Your Mental Health

You must pay attention to your emotions and your mental health to know when your mental health is not well. You must pay close attention to your emotions, your body and your mental health. If you feel or look stressed out- you should look for help. It took me years to understand this. Bottling your emotions and keeping it all in is not the answer. You must find a way, an outlet, to express this. I was always at work, and I wasn't the type to go to the gym and workout because I was at work or running back and forth with my kids between the daycare, the sports events and various activities. The boys kept me so busy in between events. They are five years apart and participated in various age groups in their group sports. I later realized I wasn't paying attention to myself. I also realized that if you keep everything inside and you don't find an outlet to express yourself, you will become emotionally and physically drained.

Be Reachable

After finishing up a long day, I would get home and get my sons situated, fed, and bathed them and prepared them for bed. I would still be up once they laid down, making sure that the house and the clothes were clean. Then I prepared everything for the next day. I also made sure to stay in a place to where my husband could get in touch with me. If I didn't answer the phone, he would be on edge. I always kept my cell phone with me so I could answer his calls.

When your spouse is deployed you want to be accessible. My husband looked forward to those calls. I am sure many soldiers want to know that their family is doing good. Social media has made this easier; it's amazing how technology has evolved. Back in the day we had limited access to phone service. He had to walk quite a distance just to use the phone. My husband would walk to a call center and purchase calling cards. Thankfully today the military has done a better job with access.

Stay Connected to Your Husband

Stay connected and send care packages and letters. Also make sure other family members have his address so they can write. You should find ways in order to keep their morale up.

Have a Financial Plan

It's important to have good communication with your spouse to make sure the bills are paid. If they are not paid, it falls back on the service member. Thankfully this was not a problem in our house, but this can be a major problem for couples. When my husband was home, he took care of the bills. When he was deployed, I took care of paying the bills. We also had a saving plan. We would save enough that when he returned, we wouldn't have to worry about money, and he could have access to whatever he needed to transition back from the field.

The army would update the wives if the soldier was deployed, they would give all of the wives a post deployment briefing. We all had to go to the unit and meet with the commander. He reviewed what should happen when a soldier returns from the field or deployment. I remember the commander ensuring we understood that a service member has been out on deployment or in the field. So, it was best to ease the soldier back into the daily functions of the house.

It's a lot of stress that the soldier goes through when they're deployed or in the field. I'm not sure if they still update the wives that way, but I always thought that was something special that helped me. Many of the soldiers would come back from being deployed, working in the field, and the wives would not have paid the bills. They wouldn't have paid the car notes or insurance, which would be all messed up when the soldier returned, and that was a problem. Before your spouse leaves:

1. Talk about what's expected before they return.

2. When they return, don't bombard them with bills and complaints.

3. Let them decompress and slowly take over.

4. Whatever they want to take over allow them the space to decide.

This line of communication worked for my husband and me. It's still working now that he is retired. He doesn't like dealing with the computer, so I take care of all that now. I don't have any problems with it. We come together when everything is done. Every household is different. You should figure out what's best for you and your husband. If you have kids, this must include all of the household's needs. It's very important that you communicate.

When we were on active duty my husband received his paychecks on the 1st and the 15th, so that gave me enough time to take care of the bills and figure out every 2 weeks what the next steps and bills I needed to tackle. To organize the bills, I would focus on what my husband had going on first then I would put things in order of importance.

We never lived beyond our means. Don't try to keep up with anybody else; make your own plans. We worked and saved and communicated. That's the best advice I can give. Make sure that you guys have communication over the expenses for the household. It runs best for me and my husband with structure and to communicate. We like to be on the same page. It doesn't work well if one person is not doing something that the other person doesn't know is going on. We had times when family members needed help and we'd talk it over and reach a solution to figure out what would be best for the family.

So, communicate early and start saving and investing early, don't wait until you get older to do it, start as early as you can, and definitely before you go out and get a vehicle or buy a home. Buy a house early because that's something that you will have paid off 25/30 years. The time frame nowadays is earlier once you go back and forth moving from state to state instead of renting. Get a starter home and later add it to your real estate portfolio. We have a house that's paid for in full and our cars are paid in full because it was a priority of my husband to make sure that the bills were paid. When we had extra money, we paid off the big-ticket items. We made sure to have a roof over our heads and run our own race. We stayed on track with paying your bills on time and tried to live within our means.

This is a behavior you must be consistent with. In the end nobody is going to pay your bills, you are going to have to pay your bills and communicate with your spouse. Keep each other in the loop even if they are out in the field, just make sure they know everything is being taken care of. I often would not bother my husband with anything that I could manage because he would leave me with the power of attorney so I could act on his behalf. I took care of everything I needed to take care of when he would get deployed or go in the field. If they do not have access to him, they will come to you.

Keep Busy

Starting off was a little difficult for me. That is when I knew I needed to get out and get a job. I had always been used to being out and working. I stayed home with our first son for six months until he was older. When we were in Cleveland, I didn't have family there, so I had to find childcare for our son since I wanted to work. I found the lady that ended up keeping him while he was a baby. Tish was her name, and she was so sweet. She kept him at her house, and I didn't have to take him to a daycare that had other kids. Tish ended up being a real great babysitter and a good friend to me. We hung out and she introduced me to going to bingo.

Before I found a job, I was lonely and had conflicting feelings. I was upset with my husband because he had a job outside the home. I learned that I couldn't lash out at him. I needed to figure out what would help me to feel better. Finding a job helped me keep my sanity. You have to find out what works for you. If working outside of the home is not an option, then you need to find a hobby. Find something to do, you need a release. I would also sew, find something to do besides going shopping and spending money. I've found several hobbies including knitting, crocheting and volunteering.

You have to find something to occupy your time so you're not sitting there upset because you're home with the kids cleaning and cooking while your husband's out. Taking care of bringing home money for the household. I didn't have access to the wives' club then. My problem was I depended on my husband to make sure I was happy. I projected what I thought he was supposed to do because I didn't have an idea on what I needed to do for myself to feel better, not be depressed and not be overwhelmed. I found myself thinking that my husband needed to help me feel better and make me happy. I wanted him to keep me from being bored and that was not his job. His job is to be a husband and a father and a provider for his family. It was my job to find out what made me happy. Earlier on when we arrived back to the states for the second time from Germany, I had to learn that lesson.

My husband was deployed three times to Korea, Saudi Arabia and Kuwait. I didn't want to be bothered with anybody during his deployments. I didn't want anybody to approach me while being out. I had a habit of putting my game face on when I left the house because I didn't want to be bothered unless I was going to my family. If I was going out shopping or out with the boys, I wore a frown on my face. In my head my protection was gone. My husband that's his job, he's a soldier. That's what soldiers do. They go out and they serve and make you feel safe, they get deployed and there's nothing you could change.

Create a Healthy Home Environment

You must make the best of whatever situation you are in. Being upset with my husband or holding resentment against him because he is a soldier is not the answer. Make your household function on a healthy level the best way you can. My household functioned on a healthy level because I found other outlets to relieve my frustrations. I did a lot of running around with our sons, and that's how I worked out my frustrations in the past. Today, I am focused on reaching my goals and completing my projects. I am being positive and saying my prayers, and having my mom to call and talk to when she was alive was a big help. I never wanted to bother her with my problems. I talked to her about whatever she needed me to talk to her about and just having her to talk to and my sisters to see them every weekend.

We found what worked for us. Having something scheduled with the kids always worked best to pass the time. You should find an activity that will make you happy and do that. Try several projects around the house. I once depended on my husband to come up with stuff to do and would get upset with him because he was tired. He'd come home and want to eat and rest. I wanted to go out. He would lie down, and I'd want to go out or drive to Savannah. We'd go to Savannah every weekend, but in between doing that, I'd want to do little things like go to the drive-in. We did things together, but he was mainly tired or at work. He would get up, go to the gym, and come back and get washed, and then we'd head into Savannah. We went to the movies or the parks to do different things for our family time. It's quite a challenge, but you must determine what's best for you.

Been There, Done That

Chapter Fourteen:
Retired Life Military Wife, Mother, Grandmother

Now that my sons have grown up, I am reinventing myself and living out old dreams. At first, it was hard, especially when our youngest son graduated from college. That was the worst- those old feelings. I was sad, and I asked what am I going to do with myself? When my adult sons moved out, I wasn't responsible for running home to prepare dinner and staying busy with their activities. After they left home, I started feeling depressed. I didn't know if I would have a life outside of being somebody's mom. I did not feel like being a wife would be enough for me, but it ended up being the perfect thing. It was exactly what I needed, and right now, my husband and I can chill out and relax.

We've always been best friends, but right now, we are at the point where he's the only person I talk to that knows exactly what I'm feeling because I tell him everything. He helps me to relax. I'm still working and don't think I will ever sit at home and not work. I'm always going to work. I have learned to take advantage of the moments and do what I love.

I believe being married to a soldier is the best job I've ever had. From the start, my husband and I jumped in with both feet. I wanted to help him grow, and in doing that, I became what I thought was a wife that made a home for my husband where he felt comfortable and safe. He is still very thoughtful and funny. We have grown together over our 38 years of marriage, from being young newlyweds full of dreams of our future together. I would not be the woman I am today if I had made different life choices. My life sometimes feels like it's a dream. Now life is quiet and peaceful, and I thank God for giving me a chance to walk in faith. I felt I had nothing to fear from leaving my family and going on what I knew would be a great adventure. When you feel strongly about something, see it through.

My husband retired at Fort Knox, and that is where we live today. I've worked for the Department of the Army Civil Services Medical and have been here since 2008. Our two sons are soldiers. My husband's retired, and I work for the Army civil services Medical.

My first cousin Juan is also retired from the military. Most of the men in my family had a military background. I remember my Uncle Vernon when he came to visit, and I told him I wanted to go into the military.

He replied, "No, I do not think that is going to work. You are not going into the military.

I asked, "Why?"

My heart was smashed because he told me he didn't want me to join the military. I wanted to go into the military so badly. After that conversation, I never revisited the idea again.

My husband and I met in grade school, and we didn't start dating until the tenth grade. From the time I met him, there was no talk of him going into the military, so it was just fate that I came across a person I would fall in love with, and his decision to join would happen later. His brothers are retired from the military. So, indirectly, I became involved with the military. I wasn't going to let Tensie Brown leave and join the military without me. This is my destiny; this is what I'm supposed to be doing.

It just blows my mind the life situations, the life experiences, and the job experiences. Going to places where people speak different languages and you're the only one who can't speak their language. I hardly even saw persons of color in Holland unless you were on a military post. We would go out to Holland, and it just blew my mind the places that I was able to visit by being associated with the military. I would not change this life. I would not change anything that has happened.

Today I continue to focus on my family, myself and try and take care of myself. I'm on a mission to put one project down, pick another up, and keep myself going. I have my grandbabies now, so I talk to them often. When they are older, they will be able to contact me if they need something. But my focus now is making sure I'm happy first and foremost. I am healthy and happy. I journal a little bit every day. Praying has also been a staple. My Mother taught my sisters and me how to pray. When we were young, we were told to say our prayers at night, give thanks for everything, and be grateful for what we had.

Try not to project negativity, negative beliefs, or feelings on the people around you. If you have a problem, say something and if you can't say something nice, then don't say anything. Stay to yourself until you change whatever negative energy you are carrying. Work it out and eliminate it because it doesn't serve a purpose; it makes you sick.

This is a perspective I acquired when my baby boy went to college. I· had to dig my heels in and put myself wholeheartedly into making myself happy and making sure my husband was good. I also have a whole new understanding and strength after living my life of my mother and her challenges of raising three girls one year apart in age. Carolyn Shirley Ann Johnson will always be my HERO. She gave us everything she had to give until she left us. This book is for my Grandkids so they know my story and they will be able to tell their story.

I started writing this book during Co-vid, and I would journal my thoughts throughout the process. I want to share those with you as a way of connecting. We often don't like to show the vulnerable side, as some may think it makes them seem weak. I think the more you can release, the stronger you are. My journal has helped me grow and reflect. I encourage you to pick a journal and write about your journey as well.

SECTION III-
MY PERSONAL THOUGHTS

"Women need real moments of solitude and self-reflection to balance out how much of ourselves we give away."

-Barbara De Angelis.

Chapter Fifteen:
My Thoughts and Prayers

My thoughts are all over the place today. My family and Miss Ann are in my thoughts. I also added Joy Robin and Jay back to my text groups. We haven't been keeping up with our communications. Mia, my supervisor, works so hard and I appreciate that.

I am also thinking about Kim Lewis. The holidays are fast approaching; I'm thankful to have God. Work is great but slow today in the mailroom. I called my oldest, DonJuan, to discuss my thoughts about writing a book.

What would I write about? The adventures of the army wife and mother of two soldiers up close and personal. I scrolled through YouTube for style inspiration. Shanique crossed my mind today, so I called her to connect again. She's the only woman I know personally who has written a book. Today is still very slow. I must go to the Commissary for a few things for Thanksgiving next week. I searched Walton Publishing House and found their website. I am on to my next adventure.

I am making a list of goals for myself. COVID made me realize time is not promised. Life is short. I cannot control others, just myself. We should be happy where we are, trust in God, do what makes us feel great, smile and communicate.

November 22, 2021, at 7:18 am

My weekend was relaxing. I purchased some seafood on Friday and went home to start my weekend. On Saturday, I watched one of me and my sister's favorite movies, the Wizard of Oz. Great childhood memories. I did some more relaxing, God is good.

On Monday morning, I went back to work. I am thankful for another day. It's slow this morning. My supervisor left the office early this morning for the day. I am working two days this week, Thanksgiving and Saturday. I started watching YouTube videos about two months ago. My mom would read her Zodiac sign and those of her children. I've always been a person to read my zodiac sign predictions.

November 23, 2021, at 1:14 pm

"On the Ocean" by K'John is playing while I am at work. "My ship is coming in." This song makes me think of my son and husband and my family. Works not busy today. I called the publishing house on Nov. 23 @ 2:00 pm and left a message for a callback.

November 29th at 7:21 am

I got back to work after five days off. Happy Thanksgiving 2021! Happy 28th birthday to our youngest son Quensie. What a blessing. I cooked my Thanksgiving meal very quietly and restfully. Thoughts of my mother and what Thanksgiving meant to her.

I received a second text from Dr. Sherrie Walton, a publisher that I came across while browsing YouTube on Noelle Randall's channel. We will talk when I get off of work today at 3:30. I'm so excited about the possibilities; thank you, Jesus. I will make my call to my publisher early. Thank God for this opportunity.

November 30th, 2021, at 8:05 am

I am listening to Oprah's ten skills that are hard to learn but will pay off forever.

1. Speaking up (public speaking)

2. Being honest with yourself

3. Focus on service

4. Having confidence

5. Listening

6. Managing your time. (Be effective and irreplaceable)

7. Stop whining

8. Stay present in the moment. Shift and refocus on something and savor it.

9. Getting enough sleep

10. Having empathy

Around the holidays, I think of my mom quite often. I cry, sing, and reflect. DonJuan texted he was proud of me. I'm proud of him, his dad, and his brother. What wonderful men I have in my life. Thank you, God. You have to stay in the light. Align your personality with what your soul came to do on earth. Life whispers to you, and you must listen.

December 1st, 2021, at 9:32 am

Believe in yourself (Denzel, Hollywood star). I spoke to Quensie last night and told him I would start writing a book about my life. He said, "I'm proud of you." Thank God, be positive, loving, grateful, kind, patient, humble, understanding, loyal, and consistent. Fall forward. Be accountable to yourself. There is a picture of Santa and helpers at work.

10:50 am

I am eating leftover greens and thinking about my childhood. I remember the early years in life at 219 Hall Street. There was love, laughter, sunshine, neighborhood friends, and the start of my love for fashion with Shirley Johnson. Her hair was the shit to me. Carolyn Carpenter is beautiful, strong, loyal, loving, and a mother of three.

Dana lived her life on her own terms. Early on, everyone wanted to be part of our lives or in our family. My husband said after a day filled with great times with family at one of our annual 4th of July celebrations nightly recaps that buying Starbucks is bougie.

How others see you isn't your concern; how you see yourself matters. I have stock in Starbucks, and I enjoy the coffee.

Stop saying I can't, ask how can I? Rich people don't work. They think poor people work. Failure is just a testing period! I am mastering my idea of being a wife and mother of superhero soldiers (people who make a difference or impact on others).

December 2nd, 2021, at 8:49 am

Five star general. My mantra is get your act together, get yourself together, get it together. Karma, your intention is always one with the law of attraction- fall forward.

December 3rd, 2021, at 8:09 am

I started work spending fellowship conversation time with Miss Mia. Failure is a sign you're moving in the wrong direction. Live out the truest and highest version of yourself. A small discussion about mail when we are at work trying to get time-sensitive information to our service members. Speak and embody incantations. Change your Physiology.

December 4th, 2021, at 2:59 pm

Not everyone was raised in love the way you were. You are one of God's creations. An original with a plan for your life. You just need to make a choice and embody and project what you feel.

December 5th, 2021, at 5:45 pm

Time does not wait (AJ + Daniel). Soulful sessions.

December 2nd, 2021,

Focus on divine provision from God. Pray for virtues, and God will provide. What do you have to change in your thinking to change your life? Desire, decide. Capricorns start a shift. In relay of one. Stop being afraid to walk and step out on faith and elevation. Pray for provision. Deliberate declaration.

December 6th, 2021, at 7:34 am

Thank you, God, for this day. I love you.

Making mental notes of information that is helping me complete my goals for myself.

Launched to Wealth. Get to know yourself and radically accept the fact of who you are. Position yourself in spaces that align with who you actually are. Focus on your own race, stay dedicated, and show up. The mind has no limitations.

December 7th, 2021, at 9:23 am

Try on different hats to find your passion. Michelle Obama said.

Practice who you want to be.

Choose excellence.

Be supportive.

Live out loud.

Empower yourself.

Own your story.

Surround yourself with positive energy.

Find something every day that moves you and you will operate at a whole different level. At some point, you have to start winning; it's on you.

December 8th, 2021, at 7:49 am

Good morning, God is good. Last night was a little uncomfortable, my arms were bothering me after I got into bed. I think my meds may have something to do with it, also caffeine and chocolate. I'm grateful to God for another day in Jesus Amen.

Oprah says. "You won't know your purpose right away. Max out your humanity. No road map, no blueprint"

Tyler Perry says, "Just love and laughter as far back as

you can remember."

December 9th, 2021, at 6:35 - 7:17 am

Running a stop sign (flashing lights.) This morning make sure you stop to check yourself. Speeding could be dangerous. Thank you, God, for another day. Great day today at work. I'm leaving early to get my booster Moderna at 13:00 (listening to Frankie-just tarot)

December 13th, 2021, at 10:37

I took Friday off, December 10th, 2021. I had a sore arm and bad pain for two days. Thank you, God I was able to come to work today. I was stopped again this morning for speeding. I need to learn the lessons of my two encounters with the law on December 9th and December 13th at 8:00 am on my way to work.

I have been listening to The Seat of the Soul by Gary Zukav. It will take several readings or listening sessions for a full understanding of what this book is saying. Intentions shape light: they set light and energy into motion. Temptation is a decoy away to see what karma would apply if carried out.

Thank God for my family, and another day. Agreement with the universe.

Chapter 24, my God my God my God. Partnership with divine intelligence.

December 14th, 2021, at 7:58 am

Happy birthday Mama. I have accepted that your body is no longer with us on earth. Thank you for always being with me and with God. Listening again to The Seat of the Soul. Evil is the absence of light.

December 15th, 2021, at 8:41 am

Christmas is upon us. My Christmas tree and some decorations are in place. I will work on getting everything up today after the work period. Working this morning makes me feel happy to serve the army family. I am still listening and learning.

December 16th, 2021, at 7:59 am

Good morning, it's Thursday. Happy birthday to Thelma.

Transfer energy into matter. Avoid unnecessary difficulties.

I am texting with Shirley, I love her so very much. Work today was great, a little slow in the end. I'm going to get a pedicure to pamper myself for my birthday, 10 days and counting down.

December 17th, 2021, at 8:08 am

God, I thank you for everything in my life.

December 20th 21 at 12:05 pm

Back to work! God, thank you for the safe arrival of

Quensie, Bella, and Aaliyah on Sunday for the holidays. I spent most of my Sunday, December 19, 2021, with them.

December 21st, 2021, at 8:39 am

The soul is the lover of our becoming. Look at where you are to accept your life and then change it appropriately as your heart tells you where to go. That's authentic power. Trust, relax, do your best, and enjoy yourself.

Text from Felicia, Uncle Vernon requires assistance at the hospital. I am unsure what he's in the hospital for. While waiting and trying to take a seat, he passed out. His blood levels were low. To God be the glory. Lay your hand on my uncle Vernon at Chandler Hospital to make a full recovery in Jesus' name, Amen.

The pain of powerlessness, feeling unlovable, is the root of the pain. We have a dual inside with dignity, soul, and personality.

December 22nd, 2021, at 8:04 am

Thank you, God! In the earth school of life, I come as one stand, but I stand as 10,000. Surviving is important thriving is elegant-Maya Angelo.

I purchased the audiobook, Proof of Heaven.

Gratitude, patience, love, contentment, and appreciation are some healthy practices for changing external triggers. You challenge and respond with a healthy part of your personality in the moment of pain.

December 28th, 2021, at 7:15 am

I was out of the office December 23-27th for the Christmas holiday and my birthday, wow. Thank you, Jesus, for my family and our health. My Uncle Vernon had to spend Christmas in the hospital. He is still dizzy when he stands. Put your hand on his body Lord to heal and rebuild his body in mind. Give him strength.

Listening to chapters 5 and 6 of The Seat of the Soul.

December 29th, 2021, at 7:52 pm

Talk to the vision. Quensie, Aaliyah, and Bella left this morning. I'm so grateful for the visit. What a blessing. Rick Ross, everyone is an author (yes). I reached out to Martika, an author of three books, to find out what her terms for publishing consisted of.

January 3rd, 2022, at 7:13 am

Happy new year, everyone. Back to work today. It's going great listening to The Seat of the Soul 2022. A blessing is an opening of a passageway. Look beyond the earth suit into the soul.

January 4th, 2022, at 7:33 am

I'm at work this morning listening again to Proof of Heaven. Two audiobooks down. I'm going to make it a point to read or listen to a book every month. Thank you, God, for the health of our family and my Uncle Vernon's full recovery. Amen.

January 5th, 2022, at 8:24 am

Thank you, God, for getting my uncle Vernon home and 100% on the mend from the hospital yesterday. At work this morning, listening to Credit is King. Also listening again to, The Seat of the soul. Thank you, God. Please give our children reverence in the eyes of their peers and subordinates in Jesus' name, Amen.

January 6th, 2022, at 7:19 am

Thank you, God, for always being there for me and my family. My mom Carolyn Shirley Ann Johnson Carpenter came home on this day in 2016. What a beautiful soul of a mother she is. It still gives me and my sister life lessons today. We are truly blessed, and miracles happen around us every day. Thank you, God.

January 10th, 2022, at 7:44 am

Thank you, God, for this day and for my family. I returned to work after snow from January 6th through 9th. The post closed on January 7, and snow melted after rain on January 9, 2022. Listening to the book Letters to my Great Grandmother, narrated by Sidney Poitier.

Saturday, I had a meeting with Martika it was a success. I'm so blessed that I met her, and I know our relationship will thrive. Amen, thank you, Jesus. Strength is multiplied when the fear is subdued in track 38. Fear will pull your strings if you let it.

January 11th, 2022, 8:26 am

Thank you, God, for waking me and all of my loved ones this morning. Thank you for the overflow. I am listening to Sidney Poitier's, Letters to My Great Grandmother. I called VA claims for my Uncle Vernon and spoke to Mr. Rivera. The forms were received, and I just needed to resend it in PDF file format, which I formatted. Done! For now.

January 12th, 2022, at 7:17 am

Thank you, God, for another day. Saying a prayer and giving thanks for everyone in our world and praying for all who need prayer this morning. Amen. Listening to The Measure of a Man by Sidney Poitier.

January 13th, 2022, at 7:12 am

Thank you, God, for another day. I started listening to Sidney Poitier, The Measure of Man. I finished the audiobook. I loved his story so much. I will be listening again.

January 14th, 2022, at 7:22 am

Thank you, God, for another day and for the health of my family. We praise you and love you. Listening to The Seat of the Soul Chapter 9 - 10. Create with reverence or with regret.

Chapter 18: Advanced human souls, the angelic Kingdom, and Angels Angel still have their will, sees, and lives in the light.

January 18, 2022, at 7:18 am

Thank you, God, I'm back at work after a three-day weekend. MLK day was Monday. I started listening to Ask, and It is Given- Part one. I started listening again to The Seat of the Soul.

January 19, 2022, at 7:32 am

Thank you, God, for another day. Bless and keep my family safe and healthy. I am truly grateful and overwhelmed by your love. Thank you, Amen. Love, compassion, and wisdom are of the soul.

January 21st, 2022, at 7:12 am

Thank you, God. I am back to work after being off. It rained heavily yesterday, so I stayed home. I am listening to The Seat of the Soul today.

January 22nd - 24th 2022

Thank you, God, for our family and our love. I stayed in all weekend coughing. The threat of the early morning cold weather started to affect my sinus. I am blessed, and God is good.

January 25th, 2022, at 7:09 am

Back to work, thank you, God, for another day. I am listening to Sidney Poitier. Thank you, God, for a quiet day. I'm still trying to recover from my days off with my cold. I am not 100% but I am feeling better.

January 26th, 2022, at 7:08 am

Thank you, God, for keeping me and my family safe and well. I love you more than life. Please bless all who I come in contact with today while at work. The lawyers called and left me a message.

So thankful to God. I started listening to Ask and It Is Given- part one. There is an avalanche of well-being at your disposal and unlimited overflow.

Thank you, God, for protecting Quensie, DonJuan, Tensie, and myself from COVID, in Jesus' name. Amen.

I want to leave for the day; thank you for a productive workday.

January 27th, 2022, at 7:29 am

Thank you, God, for another day. Thank you for my family's wonderful health and overflow of blessings. Listening to the Measure of a Man. Viewing trade station training for investment with Teri on YouTube.

January 28th, 2022, at 7:32 am

Thank you, God, for another day of blessings and

wonderful health for my family. Listening to The Measure of a Man.

January 31st, 2022, at 7:24 am

Thank you for another day of blessings and health for my family and myself. Listening to The Seat of the Soul. Happy birthday to my sister Cynthia tomorrow. Thank you, God.

You exercise your own demons.

Chapter 24 with inner faith, learn with wisdom. Awareness is the vertical path. Let go, trust and create. Take your hands off the steering wheel. Teachers and the universe are the support. Pray/ Ask /Talk/ Believe.

February 1st, 2022, at 7:50 am

Thank you, God, for another day and the blessings of great health within my family. Happy birthday to my sister Cynthia Carpenter. I am listening to The Seat of the Soul.

February 2nd, 2022, at 7:28 am

Thank you, God, for another day. Thank you for the blessing of finding Miss Teri with the 5-day challenge for investing in the stock market; Amen, thank you, Jesus.

Day 3- I started my morning working on homework for the challenge; I took notes.

February 7, 2022, at 7:04 am

Thank you, God, for another day and the health of my family. My 5-day challenge ended Friday with Miss Teri. I really enjoyed everything about trading stocks. I will enroll in her VIP course within the next one or two months. Today starts my first day under contract with my publisher Dr. Walton, I'm so excited to finally get started on one of my many books. Glory to God. Mrs. Walton emailed me today to make sure I received my welcome from her publishing office.

February 8, 2022, at 7:22 am

Thank you, God, for another day and the health of my family and myself. I spoke to Mrs. Walton last night, and I'm so glad you brought her into my life.

At work this morning I was listening to The Seat of the Soul.

February 9th, 2022, at 7:19 am

Thank you, God, for another day, and thank you for the health of my family and myself. I am leaving work early today and going to get a self-care appointment in.

February 10th, 2022, at 7:19 am

·Thank you, God, for another day. Thank you for the health of my family and myself. Great day starting my day at work at Fort Knox MEDACC, I am an author, and I am a CEO. What are people asking you for? I'm a storyteller, thank you, God.

February 11th, 2022, at 7:12 am

Thank you, God, for another day. Thank you for the health of my family and myself. I'm a little tired this morning and sleepy. I had a doctor's appointment to take labs yesterday. It's been a time going through this COVID pandemic. It's depressing and I've been eating all of the wrong things and not enough of the right. It's time to change all of that. I love you, Lord, and I know you have the last word! Amen.

February 14th, 2022, at 7:17 am

Thank you, God, for another day. Thank you for the health of my family and my health in Jesus' name. Amen.

February 15th, 2022, at 7:14 am

Thank you, God, for another day. Thank you for the help of my family and myself. It's Tuesday, and I feel great. I'm at work thinking about writing my book. Where will I start? I am listening to The Seat of the Soul today. Complaining is a form of manipulation (yes). I am listening to chapter 24.

February 16th, 2022, at 7:31 am

Thank you, God, for another day. Thank you for the health of my family and myself. It's Wednesday!

February 17, 2022, at 8:44 am

Thank you, God, for another day. Thank you for the

health of my family and myself. Computer issues at work today spilled over into this morning. Thank you for the rain today to clean away and purify. Waiting for tech support to complete my computer uploads.

February 22nd, 2022, at 7:30 am

Thank you, God, for another day. Thank you for the health of my family and myself. I returned to work after a four-day weekend. Very quiet, but my thoughts are on Quensie and his future exercise. It's in God's hands, and I pray he and his brother are covered in the blood of Jesus, Amen. My 2nd Zoom with Dr. Walton was very exciting and insightful. I will continue to focus and push through.

February 23rd, 2022, at 7:30 am

Psalms 91. Thank you, God, for another day. Thank you for the health of my family. The universe is listening to ask, and it is given to my family and myself. I pray that you protect and cover Quensie and shower him with calm and with your blood Lord Jesus. Cover DonJuan, Heavenly Father, protect and keep him safe. Amen.

Productive day today. I talked to Cynthia, to check on my printer issues. They were resolved. I must get up so I'm not running late in the morning God is good all the time.

February 24th, 2022, at 7:56 am

Thank you, God, for another day in Jesus' name. Thank you for the health of my family and my health. God is good all the time, so take the time to pay attention to the small things. I'm under contract with the universe. Listening to Ask, and it is given. We are here to experience joy. Well being is waiting outside my door.

February 28th, 2022 @ 7:07 am

Thank you, God, for another beautiful day. Thank you for the health of my family and myself. My baby Quensie started his journey yesterday. I pray that his path is blessed in all of this work, rest, and movements. Cover him with your everlasting light and bring him home safely. There is always enough. I am listening to Ask and It Is Given Part I. Life is always in motion.

A very full day of work. I caught up with my work from last week. Feeling blessed to be alive and feeling great today. I love my family. Thank you, God. I need to price tickets to Georgia and get my documents completed to send to the attorney's office.

March 1st, 2022, at 7:31 am

Thank you, God, for the health of my family and myself. I'm listening today again to Ask and It is Given. Well-being is the only stream that flows. God, thank you. Amen. I am walking in my purpose.

March 2nd, 2022, at 7:14 am

Thank you, God, for another day. Thank you, God, for the health of my family and myself. Keep Quensie and DonJuan covered in your blood in Jesus' name. Amen.

I am listening to Ask and It Is Given- part one. I spoke to Quensie yesterday, which made me happy. Thank you, God, for his safe travels.

March 3rd, 2022, at 7:18 am

Thank you, God, for another day. Thank you for the health of my family and myself. Cover Quensie and DonJuan with the blood of Jesus, also Marisha and Sean. I love you, God Amen.

March 4th, 2022, at 7:55 am

Thank you, God, for another day. Thank you, God, for the health of my family and myself. In Jesus' name Amen. Proof of Heaven chapter 35.

March 7, 2022, at 7:29 am

Thank you, God, for another day. Thank you, God, for the health of my family and myself. My weekend was relaxing. I didn't do much. I ran out Saturday to get my nails and toes done and picked up some Mary Kay from my Rep. The rest of the weekend, I relaxed and paid bills. I watched a few live streams on Instagram. Monday, back at work. I worked on my Author's University workbook notes, and I did a voice recording to forward to Mrs. Walton's assistant.

March 7, 2022, at 7:51 am

I was born in Savannah, Georgia, at the Telfair Hospital. I have two sons, and they're both in the military right now. The youngest is on the move with what's going on in the world today. He is moving away from his family. My oldest son is still at home for now with his family, but he will be on the move on Sunday. So, events are taking me back to my husband's time in the military. He's retired now. He's been retired for some years.

I have been experiencing depression. I am feeling helpless, lonely, even though my husband is with me.

I am afraid because I don't know what's going to happen to our sons. I have two daughters-in-law. I sympathize with them. I've been where they are so many times, but I would not ask for help. I needed someone to tell me it was going to be okay. Hard times are a part of life. The burden is heavier when you're home alone, taking care of your kids while taking care of yourself. The spouse at home carries the burden.

That's where I'm at now- not wanting to do too much. I have to push myself in order to move forward. I have battled with depression throughout my life. I've gone through feelings of being depressed, lonely, scared of the "what if's," just not knowing what I would do if tragedy struck me or my husband. Now I feel it for my sons just as I did when I was younger, leaving home for the first time being married.

March 8th, 2022, at 7:11 am

Thank you, God, for another day. Thank you, God, for the

health of my family and myself. Yesterday we met via Zoom with Dr. Walton for our third session; I'm feeling anxious and doubtful, thinking, do I have what it takes? Am I smart enough to do these things I dream about?

Listening to Measure of a Man, narrated by Sidney Poitier.

March 9th, 2022, at 7:24 am

Thank you, God, for another day. Thank you for the health of my family and myself. It is Wednesday and God is good.

March 14th, 2022

Thank you, God, for another day. Thank you for the health of my family and myself. Wow, what a weekend. We had a beautiful flight to Savannah, and we hit the ground running. We got a lot done, and I'm so grateful to my husband and family for the support. God is good. Amen, thank you, Jesus.

March 15th, 2022, at 8:04 am

Thank you, God, for another day. Thank you for the health of my family and myself. Today work was good, and I recorded another audio. After work I went home, fried chicken, and settled down. I called Aaliyah to check on her and Bella. They were out. Aaliyah will go to and stay until their closing date gets closer. Thinking about this past weekend, it was great seeing everyone. God is good. We got past a possible altercation in Savannah. Thank you, Jesus.

March 16th, 2022, at 7:49 am

Thank you, God, for another day. Thank you for the health of my family and myself. Happy birthday to the love of my life, my husband (Tensie Brown). Big Mama sang Happy Birthday to Tensie and walked with her walker.

I am giving birth to my dreams and praying prayers of protection. I will be traveling around July or the middle of June. My seeds are growing. Whatever you plant, I will see grow.

March 17th, 2022, at 7:19 am

Thank you, God, for another day. Thank you for me and my family's health Tensie's birthday was yesterday. It was great, thank you, God.

March 18th, 2022, at 7:14 am

Thank you, God, for another day. Thank you, God, for the health of my family and the health of myself, in Jesus' name, Amen.

March 21st, 2022, at 7:11 am

Thank you, God, for another day. Thank you for the health of my family and myself. Thank you for preparing me for all my blessings and for covering our family, Quensie, and DonJuan as they serve in the armed service. Amen.

The dispenser of fine gifts (human).

The gifts of the universe love circulating, giving, etc. They rush to the side of the givers.

Train your mind that you have something. Having will radiate more love/ happiness/ health/ joy/money. Pay bills with a sweet, wonderful attitude. Circulate energy. You are not a consumer. You are a creator. You are living as an invitation. Drive by blessings. Walk by blessings. I am in a creative mood. I recognize, celebrate, and embrace.

March 22nd, 2022, at 7:35 am

Thank you, God, for another day. Thank you, God, for the health of my family and myself. Listening day two, True Abundance, Living from the Overflow. Energy flows in and out of your being. Be thankful you can return the favor. We are generative beings. Our words are keys to unlocking the storehouse of infinite goods.

April 1st, 2022, at 7:23 am

Thank you, God, for another day. Thank you, God, for the health of my family and myself. I am worthy of all the universe has to offer. Expanding my universe. It is time. Walking in faith, taking a leap of faith. (Communication). Testimony of Personal Growth

April 4, 2022 @ 7:31 am

Thank you, God, for another day. Thank you, God, for the

health of my family and myself.

April 5th, 2022, at 8:17 am

Thank you, God, for another day. Thank you, God, for the health of my family and myself. I had my 5th Zoom meeting with Dr. Sherrie. I am falling behind with my writing. I need to change my talking points so that I can connect with my reader. I will work from my list of questions the reader may have, which are the questions I had when I began the journey.

April 6th, 2022, at 7:30 am

Thank you, God, for another day. Thank you, God, for the health of my family and myself.

April 7th, 2022, at 7:28 am

Thank you, God, for another day. Thank you, God, for the health of my family and myself. Build a career, not a moment, Vivica Fox.

April 12th, 2022, at 7:22 am

Thank you, God, for another day. Thank you, God, for the health of my family and myself.

April 13th, 2022, at 7:30 am

Thank you, God, for another day. Thank you, God, for the health of my family and myself.

April 14th, 2022, at 7:22 am

Thank you, God, for another day. Thank you, God, for the health of my family and myself. Boss energy is moving towards me. Be patient.

April 15th, 2022, at 7:21 am

Thank you, God, for another day. Thank you, God, for the health of my family and myself. In Jesus' name Amen.

April 18th, 2022, at 7:16 am

Thank you, God, for another day. Thank you, God, for the health of my family and myself. Thank you, Jesus that I decided to ride with my husband because I could see the potential in him.

April 19, 2022, at 7:16 am

Thank you, God, for another day. Thank you, God, for the health of my family and myself. Thank you, God, for the words that I need to finish my books. In Jesus' name, Amen.

April 20, 2022, at 7:36 am

Thank you, God, for another day. Thank you, God, for the health of my family and myself.

April 21st, 2022, at 7:27 am

Thank you, God, for another day. Thank you, God, for the health of my family and myself. My legacy of light is in the world but not of the world. The word wants to be written.

What do you feel? I have a legacy of light. I am the light. I am the light. It's my path alone. Trust there is a plan for my own evolution. I see myself open to receive the most. Tend to your garden the soul will lead. Leap of faith, walk in faith. Don't allow your mind to stop you. The word is waiting to be written. The story wants to be written.

April 20th, 2022

My legacy is writing. The universe is putting people in my path to manifest my future. Anyone and anything can be used in a legacy of life. It is meant to be written. Don't allow my fears and thoughts to cloud my path. Keep moving forward.

April 25th, 2022, at 7:06 am

Thank you, God, for another day. Thank you, God, for the health of my family and myself. Thank you also, Jesus, for all the words you have blessed me with to complete my books. Amen. My ships are coming in 2022. Being my own boss. My idea would turn everything around. I will bear fruit through my labor. Thank you, God, for my blessing and the blessings of my family. Amen.

April 26th, 2022, at 7:42 am

Thank you, God, for another day. Thank you, God, for the health of my family and myself. Amen. Thank you, Jesus. I ask you to provide the content and words I need to finish my books and the creativity I need to be the best version of myself in Jesus' name. Amen.

Idris Elba, Keep quiet. Let your work do the talking. I will bear fruit through my labor. Thank you, God, for the blessing of my family and myself.

April 27th, 2022, at 7:15 am

Thank you, God, for another day. Thank you, God, for the health of my family and myself. Please Lord, provide all the work that I need to complete my books in Jesus' name, Amen.

April 28th, 2022, at 7:43 am

Thank you, God, for another day. Thank you, God, for the health of my family and myself. It's Thursday, and I'm at work. I'm very grateful for my job. My life has been filled with every emotion possible. Yesterday's experience with the pain of being in a place where you have no control was frightening. Something triggered fear in my mind and I started to move quickly, trying to figure out what was happening or what I'd done to make this emotional reality.

This happens to me from time to time. Things spin out of control. I'm starting to feel it in my inner voice. I only hear it when I'm doing something that's not in alignment with my soul or what I am supposed to be doing. I've learned that I have to feel whatever emotion is needed at that moment and move past it. Focus on what's in front of me and what makes me happy and makes me feel good. I'm so grateful for my family. Moving forward with God first.

My Baby Sister

"What's happening with you today?" I asked.

Her voice sounded a little delayed. "Marion just left, and I just had breakfast. I am just planning on doing some laundry and some around-the-house cleaning. What are you doing?"

"Sitting here at work taking a break just checking with you, making sure you're taking care of yourself and not everyone else around you. You know that if something goes down with you, everything will fall apart," I said.

"I know," she said.

We started discussing our upcoming sister night at the New Edition concert and preparations for our special night out. We moved on to her telling me that she had come across a laundromat for sale on Skid Away Road, and she explained to me where it was. That led to our conversation about our joyful trips to the laundromat blocks from our house when we were younger. Oh, what a wonderful time in our lives.

"I will find out the particulars for purchasing," she said.

I replied, "Yes, that would be a great family investment. Please find out more."

With more small talk, we ended our conversation with a love you and a funny reply back and forth. She's the youngest, and I know she really misses our mom, she was her baby, and we all miss her in our own way.

Don Juan

The conversation was short, and we ended by saying we loved each other, then he was gone. So many times, I've had similar calls earlier in the morning and very late at night with my husband. Those calls are very painful, so I must help with his morale. I said to myself I will send boxes and letters weekly. This is different. The shoe is on the other foot; our sons are soldiers now. These are my babies, and I need to do what I can to help them.

Wow, what a wonderful moment. My emotions are high then low. I will need to keep my mind occupied; what a blessing our oldest son called with great news about the first house we purchased in Hinesville. "The floors are complete," he said.

We have been slowly getting the remodeling done over the past couple of years, and God said that it would be done. Amen, Thank You, God.

Quensie

My phone rang this morning at 5:15 am, which is the time my alarm goes off for me to get up for work. I walked over to answer and saw that it was Quensie calling. I haven't talked to him since last week. I called last week to check on him, but when he answered, it was a Facetime call. I could see that he was lying down, and he sounded congested. He had gotten sick and was resting.

When he called this morning, my mind went back to the many field exercises and deployments I've been through with their dad; when everything is out of your control, you cannot help them.

"Hey, Quensie," I said.

"Hello, Mom. Are you okay?"

"I'm okay; where are you?" I asked,

"Walking to work," he said.

"Walking? How far is it?"

"About a 20-minute walk."

I spoke to him about making sure to be mindful of his thoughts. His voice was strong and serious, not his usual joyful tone. I continued telling him that as long as he was okay, I and Dad would be okay.

"Your first box of goodies will go in the mail," I said, "and don't laugh when you see what I mailed."

"Why would I laugh?" he replied.

"You know me, I'm always in mama mode when it comes to my baby," I said.

Day 4 of writing (Me)

I am feeling a little afraid today of what's to come. I am missing my sons, especially Quensie. We usually talk daily; however, with him away, that's not always possible. My husband tries to do what he can to comfort me, but I still feel lonely in the back of my mind. How do I get past these feelings? I'm listening to True Abundance, an audiobook that's soothing my mind. I've been going to social media to get my mind off of feelings of loneliness. Watching others go out into the world to make things happen inspires me, and it tells me that I can do the same if I put in the work and focus on what I enjoy doing and what makes me happy.

I've spent so much time caring for and being concerned with everyone else that it's hard to focus on me. It's never too late to start changing and working on yourself; keep playing in my head. I'm happy to know that focusing on and feeling my feelings helps me find what matters and makes me feel better. I have the power to change whatever feelings I am going through, good or bad, and move through. My job gives me focus, and my creative mind helps me find ways to find happiness and gratitude.

After lunch, the second part of the day. Thank You, God, again for another day. Thank You for the health of my family and myself. We sometimes take the people in our lives for granted, and then they are gone. As I get older, my emotions become very high. I'm the type of person that will read into everything that happens to me if it affects me emotionally.

Yesterday my mind would not let me shake the feeling of loneliness, and I longed for something, a sign, a word from my sons that would make me feel better. After getting home from work, cooking a meal, and finally relaxing while watching TV and eating, I received a text from my family.

"I'm sorry to have to tell everyone this, but Kai was shot and killed near his house."

Feeling lonely became the least of my worries. A close family member had lost her youngest boy. Now my mind scrambled, trying to make sense of it all. Finally, after several phone calls, Quensie, my youngest, texted me. He had received the letter I wrote the week before, and in bold letters, he responded, "Thank you."

My answer is my heart's desire for my youngest son.

Acknowledgements

Thank You, God!

For the past few years, I have been visualizing the day that I would be able to tell a small part of my story. My family is a gift from God. Even though I am still writing, my family has always been there for me, so I would like to thank all of you, past and present. I would not be the person that I am without all of you.

Thank you to CAROLYN CARPENTER (in Heaven) and Family, NELSON CARPENTER (in Heaven) and Family, TENSIE BROWN, DONJUAN BROWN and family, QUENSIE BROWN and family, CYNTHIA CARPENTER and family, FELICIA BLUE and family, SHIRLEY JOHNSON and family, WANDA DIXON and Family, JUAN REDDY and family, VERNON JOHNSON and family, ROBBIE WHITLOCK and family, the ANDERSON family, and the CAMPBELL family. You all are a part of my village. I love you all more than you could ever know.

DANA JACQULINE YVETTE CARPENTER BROWN

About the Author

Dana Jacqueline Yvette "Carpenter" Brown

Ms. Brown is a faithful child of God who wants to help and heal all she loves. "Dana" in Arabic means Goddess of Power. A family member eloquently stated she represents a love of self and confidence. She knows who she is and always shows up for herself. Everyone that gets to experience her light never forgets that feeling. Her son says she's a "go-getter," and she has inspired him to achieve the life he has today. Many describe her as classy, refined, and a woman who goes after what she wants. She was born with these traits from her father and mother.

Made in United States
North Haven, CT
10 August 2023

40181576R00065